"The Way needs no cultivation, just do not defile. What is defilement? When with a mind of birth and death one acts in a contrived way, then everything is defilement. If one wants to know the Way directly: Ordinary Mind is the Way!"

—*Record of Ma-tsu*

# SUN-FACE BUDDHA

## The Teachings of Ma-tsu and the Hung-chou School of Ch'an

*Introduced and Translated by*
*Cheng Chien Bhikshu*

JAIN PUBLISHING COMPANY
Fremont, California

*For my mother,*
*Marija Taševa*

# *Acknowledgments*

I would like to express my gratitude to the following individuals who offered assistance during different stages of the project: Rev. Cheng-ru for helping with the translation in the early stages of the work; Ko Chi-jen and Hsü Wei-wen for helping to clarify many of the difficult passages from the original Chinese texts; Rev. Mu Soeng for contributing numerous editorial improvements; Jack Matson and Elizabeth Goreham for expressing interest in my work, and providing technical assistance towards the manuscript production; and Peter Haskel for going over the whole manuscript and offering his comments.

CHENG CHIEN

# *Contents*

# *Preface*

The present work presents primary materials on the life and teaching of Ma-tsu (709-788), who is together with Hui-neng (638-713) often considered the greatest Ch'an master in history. By extension it also presents materials on the teachings of Ma-tsu's Hung-chou school. Ma-tsu's unique approach to Buddhist practice, characterized by its immediacy, openness, and spontaneity, changed Ch'an's course of development, and served as a model for the creative developments in Ch'an teaching methods and modes of expression that took place during the later period of T'ang Dynasty (618-906), when the Ch'an school became the predominant religious force in China.

The Chinese text on which this volume's translation of the *Record of Ma-tsu* is based is the edition of *Chiang-hsi ma-tsu tao-i ch'an-shih yü-lu (Record of the Sayings of Ch'an master Ma-tsu Tao-i of Kiangsi)* from *Ssu-chia yü-lu* (*Records of Four Masters)*, a Ming Dynasty (1368-1644) collection. The division of the text into chapters and sections is not found in the original. This division, together with the chapter headings, has been suplied to faciliate better orientation and easier reading of the texts. The chapters on Ma-tsu's disciples which form the third part of this volume follow the order of their appearance in the *Record of Ma-tsu.* I have added Kuei-tsung to the list out of deference to Huang-po's opinion about his importance. Further information about the Chinese sources for the translations can be found in the Appendix, together with a list of previous English translations which contain parts of the texts translated in this volume. In doing the present translations I have to a varing degrees consulted these works and wish to express my indebtednes to them.

The purpose of this volume is to make accessible in English the teachings of Ma-tsu and his disciples to anyone interested who is unable to read the original Chinese. It is primarily meant for the general public, especially for readers who are interested in exploring the spiritual relevance of the teachings in question. The Introduction is only intended to provide basic information about the historical, institutional, and doctrinal backgrounds which were decisive in shaping the overall tone, the contents, and the ways of communicating the teachings presented in the translations, which will hopefully prevent possible misinterpretations of the texts and help the reader to better appreciate the uniqueness and the significance of the teachings presented.

In the translation I have tried to keep to the original as closely as possible. For those unfamiliar with Sanskrit and Buddhist technical terms, a glossary has been appended after the main body of the text. Some of the technical terms that do not appear frequently have been explained in the notes.

A brief note about some of the conventions followed. The transliterations from Chinese follow the Wade-Giles system. Sanskrit words which have entered the English language have been left unitalicized (e.g. sūtra, Mahāyāna). The following abreviations have been used in the notes:

| | |
|---|---|
| T | *Taishō shinshū daizōkyō*, edited by Takakusu Junjirō and Watanabe Kaigyoku. |
| HTC | *Hsü tsang ching*, a Taiwanese reprint of *Dai-nippon zokuzōkyō.* |
| CTL | *Ching-te ch'uan-teng lu*, by Tao-yüan. |

# *Part One*
# *Introduction*

# *Introduction*

The unification of China under the short-lived Sui Dynasty (590-618) paved the way for the great political, economic, and social achievements of the T'ang Dynasty (618-906), which was to become the apogee of Chinese cultural history. Under the relative peace and a stable social structure T'ang China experienced unparalleled development in the arts, crafts, and sciences, and this period has rightly been called the Golden Age of Chinese civilization.

T'ang Chinese inherited a rich Buddhist tradition which had been in their country for over a half millennium, during which time the Indian religion had been transformed and adapted to the indigenous temperament and culture of the Chinese. The foreign religion found numerous adherents at all levels of society, from poor peasants to emperors. Such was the enthusiasm of the populace for the teaching of the Buddha, or at least for the outward manifestations of it, that on numerous occasions, in the memorials presented to the throne by Confucian scholars, staggering information is found about the economic power of the Buddhist monastic community and its great influence on the ways in which Chinese society functioned. This led to a number of attempts by the state to bring the monastic community under its control and to limit its number, which if unchecked, the bureaucrats feared, would go completely out of control.

By the beginning of the eighth century most of the translation of Buddhist literature from Indian languages into Chinese was already completed, the translations done under the patronage of the Empress Wu (r. 684-705) being the last major undertaking in that direction, and all of the important sūtras were readily available in reasonably accurate translations. Besides the translations of the sūtras and the treatises of the Indian masters, there was a massive corpus of apocryphal texts composed in China, many of which became accepted as scripturally authentic in time. This process of introduction of the new religion, its gradual assimilation and adaptation, and the subsequent maturity of understanding and mastery of its doctrines, led to the creative manifestations of the Chinese religious genius, which in turn gave birth to the distinctly Chinese schools of Buddhism. Though all of these schools could trace their origins back to the Indian tradition, with different stress and emphasis on certain aspects of the doctrine they had a very distinct character of their own, which reflected native Chinese patterns of thought.

The first of these schools to be established was the T'ien-t'ai school, whose founder Chih-i (538- 597) is regarded as one of the most brilliant minds ever to appear in Chinese Buddhist history. Drawing from a great number of sūtras, Indian treatises, and the works of the Chinese monks prior to him, especially those of his teacher Hui-ssu (515-577), he created a very comprehensive system in which he brought teaching and practice, conventional and ultimate, sudden and gradual, into a harmonious unity where all distinctions lose their identity into the ultimate reality of the Middle Way. Besides arranging the scriptures in the *p'an-chiao* (division of the teachings) scheme, which can be understood both as an attempt to present a chronological arrangement of the sūtras, as well as an attempt to clarify the relationship between the ultimate and provisional teachings in the sūtras, he also compiled the various meditation techniques known during his time into his works dealing with meditation practice. From the "gradual" methods of his first work *Tz'u-ti ch'an-men* (*Gradual Ch'an [Meditation] Practice*), his works include a great variety of methods suited to various types of individuals, and lead to the "perfect sudden" practice as outlined in his monumental *Mo-ho chih-kuan (Great Calmness and Insight),* where one takes the supreme reality as the object of meditation from the beginning of one's practice.[1]

What is impressive about Chi-i's stupendous system is that while never leaving the complete teaching of the One Vehicle, in which there is nothing that is not the supreme reality, where there is no suffering to be obliterated and no Nirvana to be achieved, and where mundane and supramundane lose their identity, he still retains a very realistic outlook about the realities of the human predicament, and very clearly points to the actual practices that one has to undertake in order to truly experience the truth of the teaching in one's own being.

The importance of Chih-i for the later developments in Chinese Buddhism cannot be overstated. His works influenced the formulation of the teachings of both Hua-yen and Ch'an schools of T'ang, and his influence on the latter still awaits proper assessment. Most of the meditation manuals of the Ch'an school bear an impression of Chih-i works, and despite the efforts on the part of some of the members of the Ch'an school to cover the areas of possible influence, it still remains that Chih-i was one of the Ch'an masters that had great impact on the development of this new school.

Another important school which emerged on the Chinese religious scene not long after the formation of the T'ien-t'ai school was the Hua-yen school. Its name comes from the sūtra on which it based its doctrines: the *Avataṃsaka Sūtra,* or *Hua-yen ching* in Chinese.[2] The sūtra itself is a collection of a number of sūtras skillfully arranged together within the framework of the totalistic perspective of the one true *dharmadhātu.* The *Avataṃsaka Sūtra* can be taken as both the most consummate statement on the Buddha's enlightenment, and an unsurpassed exposition of the way of the Bodhisattva which covers all the aspects of the Buddhist Path. One of the basic themes that permeates the entire sūtra, according to the Hua-yen School, is the interdependence and interpenetration of all phenomena in the universe, in which each phenomenon is dependent on, and at the same time determining, all other phenomena. The main figures in the formulation of the teachings that are characteristic of the Hua-yen school were Chih-yen (602-668) and Fa-tsang (643-712), the reputed second and third patriarchs of the school respectively, who in their numerous writings presented their unique vision of Buddhadharma. Ch'eng-kuan (738-839), whom the tradition has taken as the fourth patriarch, was another important figure in the history of the school. In his treatises and commentaries on the sūtra he further elaborated the system which he inherited from Chih-yen and Fa-tsang, and brought it closer to the not so scholarly oriented Ch'an school. The final bridge between the two schools of Ch'an and Hua-yen came in the person of Tsung-mi (780-841), the most illustrious among the many disciples of Ch'eng-kuan. We will return to Tsung-mi in greater detail later in this Introduction.

The doctrines of the *Avataṃsaka Sūtra* and the school based on its teachings have exerted great influence on the development of the Ch'an school. Points of influence can be traced in both Ma-tsu's teachings and in the poetry of Shih-t'ou, as well as in the teachings of all the "founders" of the five schools of Ch'an that were formed during the second half of the T'ang Dynasty. This influence continued during the Sung Dynasty (960-1279), as can be witnessed in the records of the great Ch'an masters of Sung, especially in the case of Ta-hui Tsung-kao (1089-1163), who was one of the most distinguished masters of his time.

## *Formation of the Ch'an School*

Later Ch'an tradition has the Indian monk Bodhidharma (d. 532) as the putative founder of the Ch'an "school" in China.[3] A native of south India, he is said to have arrived in south China sometime towards the end of the fifth century. Legend has it that after his meting with the Emperor Wu

(r. 502- 550) of Liang Dynasty (502-557),[4] he went to north China and spent nine years at Shao-lin Monastery on Sung Mountain sitting in front of a wall. Later on he had few disciples, the most important of whom was Hui-k'o (487-593). While most of the information about Bodhidharma is of a much later origin and is not very reliable, one can get a glimpse of some of his teachings, or at least the teachings that were attributed to him, from the few texts that claim his authorship. The text most likely containing the actual teachings of Bodhidharma is *Erh-ju ssu-hsing lun (Discourse on the Two Entrances and Four Practices),* which gives an outline of two "entrances" that lead towards the Way and four basic approaches to practice. The two entrances are "entrance through the principle" and "entrance through practice"; the four practices are the practice of retribution of animosity, the practice of adaptation to circumstances, the practices of non-seeking, and the practice of concordance with the Dharma. Though it is difficult to ascertain the historical contributions of Bodhidharma, it is impossible to deny the great impact of his legend on the subsequent Ch'an history.

Hui-k'o, the main disciple of Bodhidharma, is another figure in the early history of the Ch'an school whose biography is filled with many puzzles and seeming contradictions. *Hsü kao-seng chuan (Additional Biographies of Eminent Monks)* states that his family name was Chi, and that he was a native of Hu-lao, in present-day Honan province. In his youth Hui-k'o studied the Chinese classics and Buddhist sūtras, and distinguished himself with his deep insight into their teachings. Later in life, at the age of forty, he met Bodhidharma and accepted him as his teacher. He spent six years with Bodhidharma, after which he led an itinerant life, and during his numerous travels he started teaching on his own. It is said that he received from Bodhidharma a copy of the Gunabhadra's translation of the *Laṅkāvatāra Sūtra,*[5] which Bodhidharma considered to contain the essence of the Buddha's teaching.

Almost nothing is known about Seng-ts'an, the putative third patriarch. The famous *Inscription on Trusting Mind (Hsin-hsin ming)* bears the name of his authorship, but modern scholars have seriously questioned the historicity of such an attribution.

It is only with the fourth patriarch Tao-hsin (580-651) that Ch'an tradition moves from legend to history.[6] Tao-hsin's family name was Ssu-ma, and he started studying Buddhism at the age of seven. Later on he studied the Vinaya, the *Prajñāpāramitā* tradition and the teachings of the San-lun (Three Treatises) school. He might have also practiced meditation in the tradition of T'ien-t'ai Chih-i, whose influences can be traced in the extant record of Tao-hsin's teaching.[7]

At the age of forty Tao-hsin moved to Shuang-feng Mountain in the district of Huang-mei, present-day Hupeh province. There he attracted a large following; it is said that he had five hundred students studying under him. Some of Tao-hsin's teachings have been preserved in *Leng-ch'ieh shih-tzu chi (Record of the Transmission of the Laṅkāvatāra)*[8], compiled by Ching-chüeh (683-750), which gives a version of his *Ju-tao an-hsin yao fang-pien fa-men (Expedient Teachings on the Essentials of Entering the Way and Calming the Mind)*. The main emphasis in his teaching is on the practice of meditation within the light of the understanding of the basic unity of mind and Buddha.

Tao-hsin's main disciple was Hung-jen (601-674). According to *Leng-ch'ieh jen-fa chi (Record of the People and the Teaching of Laṅkāvatāra)*,[9] compiled by Hsüan-tse (d.u.) and quoted in *Leng-ch'ieh shih-tzu chi,* his family name was Chou, and he was a native of Huang-mei. He first went to Tao-hsin at the age of seven, and stayed with him for thirty years. He is described as a noble and pure person, filled with compassion and completely dedicated to the religious life. He applied himself to his practice with great diligence, and due to his unusual talents he made an extraordinary progress. It is said that he spent his days doing monastery chores, and did his meditation at night. Upon Tao-hsin's death in 651, he moved with part of the community to Feng-mu Mountain in Huang-mei, not far from the place where Tao-hsin's monastery was located. Later the teachings of these two masters became known as the East Mountain Dharma Gate, from the name of the mountain (Tung-shan or East Mountain) were Hung-jen resided. He had many disciples, and his only instructions to them were about the practice of meditation which he considered the essence of the Path. Parts of Hung-jen's teaching can be found in *Hsiu-hsin yao lun (Discourse on the Essentials of Mind Cultivation)*.[10] His teaching can be summarized by the two Chinese characters phrase *shou-hsin* (maintaining [or guarding] the mind), the meaning of which is to maintain an awareness of the True Mind or the Buddha-nature within. Instead of trying to dispel the clouds of ignorance, one is to direct one's attention towards the absolute aspect of the mind and to let it naturally manifest itself.[11] In order to achieve this, Hung-jen exhorts the practitioners to unremittingly apply themselves to the practice of meditation.

*Leng-ch'ieh shih-tzu chi* provides a list of Hung-jen's main disciples, among whom Shen-hsiu (606?-706) is regarded as the one who received the transmission of the East Mountain teaching. Among the other disciples on the list are Lao-an (582-709), otherwise known as Hui-an, and Fa-ju (638-689), both of whom later had very successful teaching careers in northern China, and Hui-neng (638-713), who was to become known as the leader of the Southern school.

Shen-hsiu's family name was Li; he was a native of Wei-shih (in present-day Hunan). He became a monk at an early age, and in 625, at the age of twenty, he received the *bhikṣu* precepts at T'ien-kung Monastery in Lo-yang. During the first twenty-five years of his monastic life he dedicated himself to the study of the Vinaya and the sūtras, as well as the practice of meditation. In 651 he went to Huang-mei and became a disciple of Hung-jen. He stayed with him for six years, during which time he wholeheartedly committed himself to his practice under Hung-jen's instructions, and gained deep insight into his master's teaching. After a period of solitary practice, sometime during the years 676-679 he started to teach at Yü-ch'üan Monastery in Ching-chou. He gradually attracted a number of disciples, and when his reputation reached the court, Empress Wu invited him to the capital of Lo-yang. He arrived at Lo-yang in 701 where he was greeted with grand fanfare and given the greatest honors. The last years of his life were spent between the two capitals of Lo-yang and Chang-an. There he was the recipient of imperial support and the unreserved admiration of the populace. Shen-hsiu presented a comprehensive system of theory and practice in which meditation was complemented with the study of relevant texts. After his death his teaching continued to flourish in the areas of the two capitals, mostly due to the efforts of his two disciples P'u-chi (651-739) and I-fu (661-736).[12]

While some of Hung-jen's disciples were spreading the East Mountain teaching in the North, in the far south of China Hui-neng started to disseminate his unique vision of his master's teaching. Most of the sources on Hui-neng's life and teaching are not very reliable and are rather legendary in nature; critical studies of the various editions of the *Platform Sutra,* which is the basic source of information about Hui-neng, show the text to have been heavily edited and to have received numerous interpolations.[13] What follows is a basic outline of Hui-neng's life as found in this text.

Hui-neng's family name was Lu; he was born in Hsin-chou, located in the present-day Hsin-hsing district in Kwang-tung province in south China. He lost his father at a very young age and had to support his mother through manual labor. When he was twenty-five he went to East Mountain to study under Hung-jen, who immediately recognized Hui-neng's spiritual capacity. After receiving transmission from Hung-jen he spent a number of years in retreat somewhere in south China. Eventually he came out of seclusion and received the *bhikṣu* precepts form Vinaya Master Chih-kuang at Fa-hsing Monastery.[14] In 676 he settled at Pao-lin Monastery in Ts'ao-hsi, Kwangtung province, where for the next few decades till the end of his life he taught the numerus students who came to study under him. His teachings, as preserved in the *Platform Sūtra,* are relatively simple and refreshingly straightforward: among the others, he taught the simultaneous cultivation of *samādhi* and *prajñā,* as well as the doctrine of no-thought. He emphasized seeing into one's nature (*chien-hsing),* which is to be accomplished through freedom from attachment, non-abiding, and absence of (dualistic) thought.

Though from a historical perspective it is difficult to establish the exact nature of Hui-neng's teaching and his influence during his lifetime, later on he became the best known of the patriarchs, mostly due to the efforts of his disciple Ho-tse Shen-hui (670-762 or 684-758) who took it as his task to establish Hui-neng as the sixth patriarch of Ch'an. The story of Shen-hui's attack on the Northern school—which at that time didn't exist as such and the designation was Shen-hui's own creation—or rather its version as it comes to us from the Tun-huang manuscripts, forms one of the least inspiring events in the history of the Ch'an school. Whatever his motives might have been, Shen-hui eventually succeeded in establishing Hui-neng as the sixth patriarch, and from the end of the eight century on, the Ch'an school came to be identified with the followers of Hui-neng.

Among the disciples of Hui-neng the best known are Nan-yang Hui-chung (d. 775), Yung-chia Hsüan-chüeh (665-713), Nan-yüeh Huai-jang (677-744), and Ch'ing-yüan Hsing-ssu (660-740). Hui-chung rose to great prominence when, in 761, Emperor Su-tsung (r. 756-763) invited him to the capital where he taught till the end of his life. The next emperor, Tai-tsung (r. 763-780), gave him the title "National Teacher," and in later Ch'an literature he is referred to as National Teacher Chung. Yung-chia spent very little time with the Sixth Patriarch and it is obvious from the extant records that he already had a very profound experience before he went to see the Sixth Patriarch, who merely confirmed his understanding. He is best remembered by his composition the *Song of Enlightenment (Cheng-tao ko)*, which has ever since been one of the most popular statements on the Ch'an experience. Not much is known about Huai-jang and Hsing-ssu. Their primary significance lies in the fact that they were teachers of Ma-tsu Tao-i (709-788) and Shih-t'ou Hsi-ch'ien (700-790),[15] respectively. We will return to Huai-jang again bellow.

Besides the above mentioned schools, during the eighth century there were other collateral branches of the Ch'an school which flourished at different locations in China. Two of them were the Niu-t'ou school and the Szechwan school. The Niu-t'ou school considered Fa-jung of Niu-t'ou Mountain (594-657) as its founding teacher and claimed that he received transmission from the fourth patriarch Tao-hsin—a claim that is open to a lot of doubts.[16] In the teaching of the Niu-t'ou school there can be found influences from the T'ien-t'ai school, the *Prajñāpāramitā* literature and the San-lun school, especially in its extensive use of negation and emphasis on emptiness, as well as a lot of similarities with the teachings of the Southern school.

The most distinguished representatives of the Szechwan school were the Korean monk Wu-hsiang (694-762), and Wu-chu (714-774) from Pao-t'ang Monastery in Cheng-tu. The hallmark of its teaching was the doctrine of *wu-nien,* or no-mind, which was also the central concept of the Southern school, or at least of its Shen-hui faction. The main sources for a reconstruction of the teachings of the school are *Li-tai fa-pao chi (Record of the Dharma-treasury Through Generations)*,[17] and the writings of Tsung-mi.[18] This school has been criticized for its extreme position and its unqualified emphasis on non-duality which leave themselves open to antinomian interpretations. More will be said about the Ch'an movement in Szechwan bellow.

Besides these schools, Tsung-mi also mentions the Ch'an school of Nan-shan whose founder was Hsüan-shih (d.u.), a disciple of the Fifth Patriarch. This school practiced a form of contemplation of Buddha, in which verbal repetition of the Buddha's name was used to gradually induce a relinquishment of mental conceptions, so that the mind will be infused with Buddha who will then be manifested in each thought.[19]

As can be seen from this short historical summary, Ch'an at the beginning of the eighth century included a variety of different schools, all of which had developed their own systems and methods of practice. These loosely-connected groups of monks were closely correlated through a great deal of mutual influences and free exchange of ideas. Instead of emphasizing the divisions and sectarian feelings that characterize some of the works dating from that period, which seems to be the direction that most of modern scholarship have taken, a more meaningful approach towards understanding early Ch'an history might be to return to the teachings of its great masters. They provide a well-defined analysis of the possible distortions of the teaching and clearly expose the fallacy of establishing separate schools and indulging in sectarian controversies. The works that try to establish different lineages claiming supremacy for their own only reflect some of the worldly attitudes and sentiments that surrounded the masters, and are only conditioned perceptions motivated by sectarian rivalry and desire for prestige and predominance. None of the great masters tried to establish any separate school: Bodhidharma did not establish a separate Ch'an school; Hui-neng did not establish the Southern school; neither Lin-chi nor Tung-shan had anything to do with the establishment of what came to be known as Lin-chi and Ts'ao-tung schools.[20]

In connection with this, it might be useful to remind ourselves of the words of Fa-yen Wen-i (885-958), who shared the same fate with many other masters when after his death some of his disciples proclaimed him a founding master of a school that carried his name.[21]

> The Patriarch did not come to this land in order to transmit any teaching—he only directly pointed to the human mind so that people can perceive their nature and become Buddhas. How could there be any sectarian doctrines to be upheld?
>
> Even so, there were differences in the teaching styles of the later masters which were open to change in accord with situations. Like the two masters Hui-neng and Shen-hsiu who both [studied under] the same teacher, but had different understanding of his teaching. That is why people created the labels of Northern and Southern schools. After Hui-neng, Hui-ssu and Huai-jang continued the teaching. Hui-ssu was the teacher of Shih-t'ou, and Huai-jang was the teacher of Ma-tsu. From these two masters came the various branches, each of which flourished in a particular area. But the true origin of all the teachings is not to be put within a historical context . . . [All of the great masters] had distinct teaching styles, and when the teaching was passed to their disciples some of them started forming factions. Not realizing the original reality, they started to accuse each other and engage in disputes. They are unable to distinguish black from white, and do not understand that the Great Way has no position and that all streams of Dharma are of the same flavor. They are very much like someone trying to paint empty space, or like someone trying to pierce iron or stone with a needle.[22]

## *The Life and Teaching of Ma-tsu*

Ma-tsu was born in 709 in Han-chou in the southern part of the remote province of Szechwan, in the far west of

China on the border with Tibet.[23] There is no other information about his family background except that his family name was Ma. Like most Ch'an masters he left home while still very young and entered the monastic order as *śrāmaṇera,* or novice monk. His first teacher was Ch'u-chi (665-732), whose lay surname was T'ang, and who was thereby known as Venerable T'ang. Ch'u-chi in turn was a disciple of Chih-shen (609-702), one of the Fifth Patriarch's disciples whose name appears in the list of Fifth Patriarch's main disciples in *Leng-ch'ieh shih-tzu chi*. Tsung-mi in his commentary on the *Perfect Enlightenment Sūtra,* the *Yüan-chüeh ching ta-shu ch'ao,* provides the information that Ma-tsu also studied under Ch'u-chi's disciple Venerable Kim (684-762),[24] a Korean monk who is better known under his Dharma-name Wu-hsiang. Both Ch'u-chi and Wu-hsiang were among the leading figures in the Ch'an movement in Szechwan in the first half of the eighth century, and the important fact that Ma-tsu studied under both of these monks is of great help in understanding the possible influences on the development of his teaching style. According to *Li-tai fa-pao chi,* Wu-hsiang taught the "three phrases" which he called the "all-inclusive teaching." The three phrases are no-remembering (*wu-i*), no-thought (*wu-nien*), and no-forgetting (*mo-wang*);[25] they were taken by Wu-hsiang to correspond to the three main aspects of traditional Buddhist practice: *śīla, samādhi,* and *prajñā.*[26] Tsung-mi describes this teaching as follows:

> As to the three phrases, they are no-remembering, no thought, and no-forgetting. [Their function is] to cause the mind to abandon the memory of past events and to stop worrying about the vicissitudes of the future, so that it will always conform to this understanding without any confusion or mistake. This is what is called no-forgetting. Again, not remembering external objects and not thinking of the mind within, one should cultivate this without any attachment. The

> order of *śīla, samādhi,* and *prajñā* corresponds to the order of the three phrases. Though they used many expedients in their teaching, in their essential meaning they were all included within the three phrases.[27]

The teachings of the Szechwan school were known for their emphasis on non-duality, spontaneity, and non-reliance on the external forms of religious practices, all of which can be found in Ma-tsu's teaching. That might be taken to imply that he was considerably influenced by his early teachers and that this influence was carried throughout his life. It might be also mentioned that he spent more time as a monk in Szechwan, presumably with his teachers, than with Huai-jang who is traditionally considered the teacher from whom he received transmission. However, it is difficult to ascertain exactly how much time he spent with these two monks, since he might have studied with some other teachers in Szechwan. Also the amount of time spent with a particular teacher is by no means a clear indication of the extent of that teacher's influence, especially in the early years of one's monastic life.

In 738 Ma-tsu received the *bhikṣu* precepts from Vinaya Master Yüan of Yu-chou province,[28] and soon after that he left Szechwan for central China. The next available information after his ordination is that during the K'ai-yüan period (713-742) he stayed at Ch'üan-fa Monastery in Heng-yüeh, in present-day Hunan, engaged in the practice of meditation. This implies that he moved to Heng-yüeh sometime between 738 and 742. The fact that he enthusiastically dedicated himself to the practice of sitting meditation, which seems to have been neglected by his teachers in Szechwan, coupled with the fact that he later referred to the *Laṅkāvatāra Sūtra* as a scriptural support of his teaching and as the sūtra that was transmitted by Bodhidharma, may be taken to indicate that during that period Ma-tsu was influenced by the teachings of the so-called Northern school, which at that time was flourishing in the North.[29] The practice of sitting in meditation and the connection with the *Laṅkāvatāra Sūtra* are traditionally considered to be the two main characteristics of the Northern school that are said to stand in sharp contrast to the rejection of sitting meditation and a reliance on the *Diamond Sūtra* by the Southern school. However, the surviving texts that contain the teachings of the Northern school bear very little reference to the *Laṅkāvatāra,* which seems to suggest that the sūtra was not very much used by the Northern school.[30] It is also not certain if Hui-neng really championed the *Diamond Sūtra,* or whether that was another of Shen-hsiu's inventions; what is most likely is that instead of completely rejecting any form of meditation practice, Hui-neng criticized the view that enlightenment can be attained by meditation, which by no means implies that meditation is not useful in preparing the conditions that are necessary to bring about the experience of sudden enlightenment.

During his stay in Heng-yüeh Ma-tsu met Huai-jang; the famous story of their meeting can be found in the translation of the *Record of Ma-tsu* which forms part two of this book. However, while the *Record* states that Huai-jang encountered Ma-tsu while the latter was practicing meditation at Ch'üan-fa Monastery, according to Tsung-mi it was Ma-tsu who paid a visit to Huai-jang while on a pilgrimage. According to Tsung-mi's version the two had a discussion about the teaching, and after Ma-tsu realized that Huai-jang's understanding was superior to his own, he decided to become his disciple.[31]

There is very little information about Huai-jang, and the authenticity of that which is available have been brought in question. We are told that he left home at the age of fifteen and, after receiving the *bhikṣu* precepts some years later, he went to study with Lao-an, one of the disciples of the Fifth Patriarch (mentioned earlier in this Introduction). Lao-an sent him to his Dharma-brother Hui-neng who was teaching in the South. The story of Huai-jang's meeting with the Sixth Patriarch is recorded in the *Transmission of the Lamp* as follows:

> The Patriarch asked him, "Where are you coming from?"
>
> The Master (i.e Huai-jang) said, "I am coming from Sung Mountain."
>
> The Patriarch asked, "What is it that has come?"
>
> The Master said, "To speak of it as something does not reach it."
>
> The Patriarch asked, "Can that be cultivated or testified to?"
>
> The master said, "It is not impossible to cultivate it or to testify to it, it is only that it cannot be defiled."
>
> The Patriarch said, "It is this very thing that cannot be defiled what all the Buddhas guard and think of. You are thus, and so am I. The Patriarch Prajñātāra of India[32] had made a prophecy that from beneath your feet a horse will appear that will stamp to death the people in the world. Keep this in your mind; you don't have to speak of it soon." The Master's mind opened and he understood [the Patriarch's] meaning.[33]

According to the *Record of Ma-tsu*, Ma-tsu spent ten years with Huai-jang, during which time he received Huai-jang's instructions and refined his practice. After leaving Huai-jang sometime around 750, he spent over two decades in various locations in the area of the present-day Fukien and Kiangsi provinces.[34] We have very little information about this period of his life, but it seems safe to assume that he continued his practice and taught those who came to him for guidance. That was a time when most of China experienced great social unrest following the An Lu-shan rebellion of 755. The unstable social conditions lasted till 763, and initiated changes in the social structure and shift in the centers of power that signaled the gradual decline of T'ang Dynasty.

Sometime during 776-779 Ma-tsu took permanent residence at K'ai-yüan Monastery in Chung-lin,[35] in present-day Kiangsi province. From then on students started coming to him in ever increasing numbers, and he wholeheartedly responded to their enquiries, offering his guidance along the Path to all who came to him. His teaching career at K'ai-yüan Monastery lasted for only about ten years and ended with his death in 788. The number of his close disciples who gained deeper understanding of Ch'an was one hundred and thirty-nine—or eighty-four, depending on the source—more than any other Ch'an master in history.[36]

The movement initiated by Ma-tsu later came to be known as the Hung-chou school, after the name of the area where Ma-tsu and most of his disciples taught. During the ninth century many of the Hung-chou school's monks spread Ma-tsu's teaching across China, and together with the illustrious Shih-t'ou he is regarded as the most important master for the development of the late T'ang schools of Ch'an.

Ma-tsu's relationship with Shih-t'ou is very interesting. Though there is no evidence that the two masters ever met, it is obvious that they held each other in high esteem. Many of the important Ch'an monks studied with both masters. Very often one of the masters will advise a particular disciple to go to the other master and study with him. As the saying from that period goes, "Ta-chi was the master in Kiangsi; Shih-t'ou was the master in Hunan. Those who were wavering and didn't go to see these two great teachers were considered completely ignorant."[37] With Shih-t'ou and Ma-tsu Ch'an entered a new phase of development. The meditation instructions of Tao-hsin and Hung-jen, and Hui-neng's simultaneous cultivation of *samādhi* and *prajñā* gave way to a new teaching style that was refreshingly open and direct. Many of the teaching devices that later on came to be identified with the Ch'an school—such as shouts, blows, enigmatic questions—were first used by Ma-tsu. This change in teaching style initiated by Ma-tsu and his followers, coupled with the change in the literary format used to record their teachings, have even led some to perceive discontinuity between the Ch'an of Hui-neng and Ma-tsu. Anyhow, from the beginning of the ninth century on, all Ch'an masters were considered spiritual descendants of Ma-tsu and Shih-t'ou.

The philosophical foundation of Ma-tsu's teaching is mainly based on the *tathāgatagarbha* doctrine. The scriptural support of the *tathāgatagarbha* teaching can be found in such texts as the *Śrīmālā*, the *Tathāgatagarbha*, the *Sūraṅgama*, and the *Perfect Enlightenment Sūtras*, as well as the *Avataṃsaka Sūtra*, especially its "Appearance of the Tathāgata" chapter, and in the *Ratnagotravibhāga*, which is the only extant Indian *śāstra* which gives more detailed treatment to this influential doctrine. The *tathāgatagarbha* is also found in the *Laṅkāvatāra Sūtra* and the *Awakening of Faith*, but in these two texts it is combined with the Yogācāra doctrine of *ālayavijñāna*. The *tathāgatagarbha* doctrine represents a tendency in Buddhism to describe reality in more positive terms. The *tathāgatagarbha*, which is sometimes translated as the "womb of Buddhahood," is conceived of as an indestructible essence present in all sentient beings which is the cause for both the ultimate reality and the realm of phenomenal appearances. This essence, or "seed," is described as being neither existent nor non-existent. It is the suchness of things, or when spoken of in more apophatic terms, their emptiness.

The *tathāgatagarbha* doctrine alleges that all living beings are endowed with the True Mind, which is fundamentally enlightened and pure by nature, and is only adventitiously covered with defilements. In his *Ch'an-yüan chu-ch'üan-chi tu hsü* (*Preface to the Collection of all Explanations on the Source of Ch'an*) Tsung-mi explains the *tathāgatagarbha* doctrine in the following manner:

> This teaching says that all sentient beings posses the true mind of emptiness and quiescence, whose nature

> is without inception fundamentally pure. Bright, unobscured, astute and constantly aware, it constantly abides to the end of time. It is called Buddha-nature; it is also called *tathāgatagarbha* and mind-ground. [Because] from time without beginning it has been concealed by false thoughts, [sentient beings] cannot realize it, and thereby experience birth and death. The Supremely Enlightened, feeling pity for them, manifests in the world to proclaim that all dharmas characterized by birth and death are empty, and to reveal the complete identity of this mind with all the Buddhas.[38]

This True Mind has also been described by Huang-po Hsi-yün (d. 850), who is traditionally regarded as Ma-tsu's grandson in the Dharma, as follows:

> This mind has from the very beginning been independent of birth and death. It is neither green nor yellow, without form and characteristics. It does not belong to either existence or nothingness, and it cannot be reckoned as either young or old. It is neither long nor short, neither large nor small. It transcends all limitations, words, and traces. It is just this very thing—if you stir a thought, you miss it. It is like empty space, without limits, beyond conceptualization. It is only this One Mind that is Buddha, and Buddha is not different from sentient beings.[39]

While in its essence the True Mind, or the Buddha-nature, is beyond thoughts and is devoid of any signs, in response to things it can manifest itself in a variety of ways. It is this dynamic aspect of the True Mind that is of paramount importance to Ma-tsu, according to whom the realization of this mind, and thereby enlightenment, is to be achieved through recognizing it in its function. So, the Way is not some abstract metaphysical principle: our very words, thoughts, and actions are its function. Reality is not to be sought apart from daily life. Reality is present in everything—is everything—and it is only due to our ignorance that we fail to realize this. Therefore, "all living beings have since beginningless *kalpas* been abiding in the *samādhi* of the Dharma-nature," and all ordinary activities are the Dharma-nature. As Ma-tsu is quoted by Yung-ming Yen-shou (904-975) in his *Tsung-ching lu (Record of the Mirror of the Teaching)*: "If you wish to know your mind, this very one that is talking now is your mind. This is what is called the Buddha, and is the true *dharmakāya* of the Buddha, and is also called the Way."[40]

However, due to beings "not knowing how to return to the source, they follow names and attach to forms, from which confusing emotions and falsehood arise, thereby creating all kinds of karma." It follows that "ignorance is to be ignorant of one's original mind," and enlightenment consist in simply "awakening to one's original nature."

Since the True Mind is already present in all beings, it is not something to be approached through cultivation, which implies a process of gradual progress through stages, and inevitably leads to dualistic thinking which is the very cause of ignorance. And yet, the painfully obvious fact of our ignorance and suffering makes it plain that there is need for some form of cultivation. "To attach to original purity and original liberation, to consider oneself to be a Buddha, to be someone who understands Ch'an, that belongs to the way of those heretics who deny cause and effect, and hold that things happen spontaneously," says Ma-tsu's disciple Pai-chang Huai-hai (749-814).[41] Ma-tsu himself points that "if one says that there is no need for cultivation, then that is same as ordinary [ignorant] people."[42] While the Way is not to be approached through cultivation, its realization is not outside of cultivation.

Cultivation, as Ma-tsu sees it, consists of not defiling our true nature. The defilements that are referred to are the mental tendencies of bifurcating reality into conflicting opposites of good and bad, right and wrong, worldly and holy; the defilements consist in thinking in dualistic terms and acting in contrived ways, in creating all kinds of views and opinions, desires and attachments, and regarding all of them as real. So, instead of trying to remove defilements which are themselves illusory, one has simply to realize their empty nature. This realization is correlated with letting go, which interrupts the habitual pattern of conceptual proliferation and lets the brightness of the original nature manifest itself.

The phrase used by Ma-tsu which best describes this kind of approach to cultivation is "Ordinary Mind is the Way." Ordinary Mind is the mind that is free from the notions of good and bad, right and wrong, permanent and impermanent, worldly and holy; it is the mind that is free from activity, from grasping and rejecting. The following dialogue between Nan-ch'üan (747-834) and his disciple Chao-chou (778-897) well illustrates the meaning of "Ordinary Mind":

> One day Chao-chou asked Nan-ch'üan, "What is the Way?"
>
> "Ordinary Mind is the Way," said Nan-ch'üan.
>
> Chao-chou asked, "Can it still be approached?"
>
> Nan-ch'üan said, "If you try to approach it, you go away from it."
>
> Chao-chou further asked, "If we do not approach it, how can we know that it is the Way?"
>
> Nan-ch'üan replied, "The way does not belong to knowing or not knowing. Knowing is false awareness; not knowing is neutral. If without any doubt you truly penetrate the Way, then it is like empty space, vast and open. How can then there be any quibble about right and wrong?"[43]

The teaching of Ma-tsu is considered to belong to the tradition of "sudden enlightenment" which, in the eyes of some of its followers, stands against the tradition of gradual enlightenment. As its name suggests, this tradition held that enlightenment comes in a sudden fashion and does not involve any gradation of stages. With its emphasis on non-duality this tradition often found itself at odds when it came to discussing any methods of cultivation. Since cultivation must involve some progression and reliance on verbal explanations, according to that line of thought, it inevitably leads to the realm of duality. For this reason in the writings that are associated with this school there is a marked tendency towards elocutionary purity, where all forms of verbal formulation are eschewed, including any instructions about practice. However, the fact that practical advice about day-to-day cultivation is something that is usually lacking in the records of the masters of this tradition does not necessary means that it was not given by them. In the records of Ma-tsu's Hung-chou school there are instances with very clear "gradual" tinge, like the story related in dialogue 7 of this volume's translation of the *Record of Ma-tsu,* in which Shih-kung compares his cultivation to tending an ox. The same allegory also appears in the teachings of Pai-chang and his disciple Ta-an.[44] Again, Ma-tsu himself refers to nourishing the "womb of sagehood," a reference to the gradual development of the stages that constitute the Bodhisattva path,[45] and also encourages his disciples to keep pure *śīla* and try to accumulate wholesome karma.[46] In the record of Pai-chang there is the passage: "One's study should be like washing dirty clothes; the clothes are originally there, the dirt is from outside."[47] This is analogous to the practice of gradually removing defilements and returning to the original purity of the self-nature. Perhaps the most clear explanation of the place of gradual cultivation in Ma-tsu's Hung-chou school comes from the record of Kuei-shan Ling-yu (771-853), the great disciple of Pai-chang:

> There was a monk who asked the Master, "Does a person who has had sudden awakening still need to continue with cultivation?"

> The Master said, "If one has true awakening and attains to the fundamental, then at that time that person knows for himself that cultivation and non-cultivation are just dualistic opposites. Like now, though the initial inspiration is dependent on conditions, if within a single thought one awakens to one's own reality, there are still certain habitual tendencies that have accumulated over numberless *kalpas* which cannot be purified in a single instant. That person should certainly be taught how to gradually remove the karmic tendencies and mental habits: this is cultivation. There is no other method of cultivation that need to be taught to that person."[48]

In looking for possible reasons for the apparent lack of expedient means in the extant records of the teachings of the Hung-chou school, it might be useful to remind ourselves of the audience to whom the teaching was directed. As the records make it clear, most of the teachings were received by monks who were familiar with the basic Buddhist practices and (ideally) had good command of the doctrinal teachings. We are also not in a position to know the exact details of the various instructions that were given to students due to the very limited material at our disposal, most of which was not written by the masters themselves and was edited a number of times. It seems that the basic practices of worship, study, precepts, and meditation were all too familiar to be regarded as something that was necessary to be recorded. This is clearly stated by Pai-chang:

> If one were to speak to deaf worldlings, then they should be told to leave home, keep the precepts, practice meditation, and study wisdom. To worldly people who are beyond ordinary measures—like Vimalakīrti[49] and Bodhisattva Fu[50]—one should not speak in that way. If one is speaking to *śramaṇas*, they have already committed themselves to the

> religious life[51] and the power of their *śīla, samādhi,* and *prajñā* is already complete. If one still speaks to them in that way, that is called untimely speech, because it is not appropriate to the situation; it is also called improper talk. To *śramaṇas* one should explain the defilement of purity; they should be taught to leave all things, whether existent or non-existent, to forsake cultivation and attainment, and also let go of the very notion of forsaking. If *śramaṇas* in the course of their abandonment of defiling habitual tendencies cannot let go of the diseases of greed and hatred, they are also to be called deaf worldlings. In such a case they should also be told to practice meditation and study wisdom.[52]

The above passage makes it explicit that the strong foundations in ethical conduct and meditation practice are the most basic standards for monks, and due to their wide acceptance and familiarity they need not be particularly emphasized. Instead, monks, and those layman who are sufficiently advanced, should be taught the more subtle teaching that directly points to the realm beyond assertion and denial, cultivation and attainment. However, if one does not have strong foundation in precepts and meditation, then that person needs first to dedicate himself or herself to the strict practice of keeping precepts and development of mental clarity, without which one is bound to go astray. The same opinion was also expressed by Kuei-shan who maintained that only those students who have great capacity and determination should dedicate themselves to the practice of Ch'an. For the majority of practitioners he recommends cultivation of more conventional Buddhist practices like observing precepts, study and preaching of the scriptures, and investigation of the doctrinal teachings.[53]

The teachings of Ma-tsu and all other Ch'an masters need to be understood in the context of the Buddhist tradition at large. As even a superficial reading of their records will reveal, most masters were very well versed in the scriptures and used doctrinal formulations very freely. In the relatively short text of the *Record of Ma-tsu* there are quotations from the *Laṅkāvatāra Sūtra,* the *Vimalakīrti Sūtra,* the *Avataṃsaka Sūtra,* the *Sūtra of the Buddha's Names,* the *Fa-chü ching,*[54] the *Awakening of Faith,* as well as allusions to the *Sūraṅgama Sūtra,* the *Mahāparinirvāṇa Sūtra,* and the *Lotus Sūtra.* This can hardly be taken to support the widely held opinion that the Ch'an masters after Hui-neng discouraged study of the sūtras. They certainly pointed to the danger of "getting stuck in the net of scriptural explanations," which is a statement against a wrong use of the scriptures, of which there was plenty in T'ang China, not against the scriptures themselves. That ultimate reality is not something that can be verbally explained is a basic teaching of all schools of Buddhism, and the dangers of becoming too attached to the literal meaning of the teachings is frequently pointed out in the scriptures. All of the teachings of the Ch'an school can be found in the sūtras, or even in one sūtra: the *Avataṃsaka Sūtra.* Few parallels might be quoted here. Corresponding to the famous saying of the Ch'an school "mind is Buddha," there are the following passages in the sūtra:

> The knowledge of the *Tathāgata* is also thus—boundless and unobstructed, universally able to benefit all sentient beings, it is fully present within the bodies of sentient beings. But those who are ignorant, prone to false thinking and attachments, do not know this, are not aware of it, and thus do not obtain benefit. Then the *Tathāgata,* with his unobstructed pure eye of knowledge, universally beholds all sentient beings in the *dharmadhātu,* and says, "Strange! How Strange! How can it be that although all sentient beings are fully possessed of the knowledge of the *Tathāgata,* because of their ignorance and confusion,

> they neither know nor see that? I should teach them the noble path, thus enabling them to forever leave false thoughts and attachments, and perceive the vast knowledge of the *Tathāgata* within themselves, not different from that of the Buddhas.[55]

and elsewhere,

> As mind is, so is the Buddha;
> As the Buddha is, so are living beings.
> One should know that the Buddha's and mind's
> Essential nature is boundless.[56]

About "neither mind nor Buddha," we find in the sūtra:

> Living beings falsely discriminate,
> That is the Buddha, this is the world.
> For the one who comprehends the Dharma-nature,
> There is neither Buddha nor world.[57]

and about non-attachment to verbal explanations:

> [Bodhisattvas] receive and uphold all the teachings, and yet do not give rise to attachment to the teachings....Bodhisattvas think, "I should contemplate *dharmadhātus* as illusions, all Buddhas as shadows, all Bodhisattvas as dreams, the Buddha's teachings as echoes, all worlds like illusions...."[58]

While perhaps there might not have been much novelty in the contents of the teachings which the Ch'an school used to convey its vision of Buddhadharma, what sharply distinguished it from the other schools of Chinese Buddhism was the way those teachings were presented and applied in the course of religious cultivation and daily life. The masters used the teachings in a free and uncontrived way with the sole purpose of helping their students to break through their delusions and attain liberation. That is why their words are very alive and full of force, penetrating directly into the heart of the seeker. This practical emphasis on practice and awakening as the whole meaning of religious life is nowhere felt as strongly as in the records of the Ch'an masters. There is very little space in them for abstract theories and useless theoretical speculations; all their energy is instead directed towards leading the individual to fully experience the infinite wisdom of the Buddhas in his or her body. Of course, all other schools of Chinese Buddhism do emphasize practice. It is only that sometimes their elaborate systems tend to pose the danger of getting too attached to the words and concepts that are used to point to the realm beyond words and concepts, and to thereby forget the original intention behind all those profound theories: the need to use them.

## *The Monastic Tradition*

Within the Buddhist tradition all the various teachings that have been expounded by the Buddha and all the enlightened teachers are considered mere expedients that are used to counteract certain unwholesome tendencies which are detrimental to the Path, and to bring about positive qualities which enable one to break through the clouds of ignorance and let the sun of wisdom shine, illuminating the world and bringing benefit to all living beings. The unfixed nature of the teachings is very much emphasized throughout all traditions, as is well illustrated by the famous simile of the raft.[59] The value of all teachings and the practices based on them is purely instrumental; when the river of *saṃsāra* has been crossed, the verbal teachings are left behind, and one merges with the inconceivable state of unobstructed liberation that is completely beyond the realm of the dualistic mind. The non-dogmatic nature of Buddhist practices and experience is nowhere emphasized as much as in the records of the Ch'an school. While other schools did establish certain doctrines to guide the students, temporary and flexible as they may be, most of the Ch'an masters after Ma-tsu avoided using any particular set of teachings, and instead responded to the needs of particular person or situation in an unconstrained and spontaneous way, relying on the power of their own insight. As Lin-chi says, "I have no teaching to give to people; all I do is untie knots." Within Ch'an after Ma-tsu the teaching can only be understood against the relationship between the master and the student, and it is this dynamic interaction between the two that gives vitality to the teaching. For this very reason, in order to gain better insight into the real meaning behind the words and actions of the masters, we have to acquaint ourselves with the social, cultural, doctrinal, and institutional context in which the teaching was given, the people to whom it was given, their values and conditioning. This is an especially important consideration in the West, whose culture is based on very different assumptions and values from the culture and institution that gave birth to the Ch'an teaching in T'ang China.

A good example of the importance of considering the context in which particular teaching was given in order to understand its purport is the already mentioned story of Ma-tsu's meeting with Huai-jang. Whether we understand the statement made by Huai-jang that sitting in meditation is as likely to make one a Buddha as polishing a brick is going to turn it into a mirror as a categorical rejection of meditation practice, or as an instruction about the way meditation should be practiced, will depend on the institutional setting in which the event occurred. If meditation was part of the daily practice of the monks, and if Huai-jang himself participated in it, than it can be better appreciated as a statement about the right attitude with which meditation should be approached. On the contrary, if the monastic life at Huai-jang's monastery precluded any form of meditation practice, then it might be understood as a denial of meditation practice per se.

Reading of Ch'an texts easily brings to notice that what figures most prominently is the monastic character of the tradition. The vast majority of Ch'an practitioners who gained deeper insight into Ch'an were monks; it follows then that the monastic character of the tradition is a factor that should be given due consideration.[60] Unfortunately very often that is not the case. Many of the works on Ch'an (and especially Zen) in the West tend to overlook this aspect, and the result is an inadequate understanding of the tradition crippled by a false assumption that the limited range of views and perceptions that we have been conditioned to by our culture are universal in character, and are equally valid in the context of Ch'an. Much has been made of the apparently iconoclastic, rebellious, anti-institutional tendencies in Ch'an without considering that the particular utterances were given to monastic communities, in the context of which they assume completely different meaning than the one imposed on them by those not familiar with the values and the principles that governed the life in the community.[61] What follows is a short description of the monastic institution in T'ang China, which, I hope, will help towards a better appreciation of the Ch'an teaching.

Ma-tsu and the other masters who carried the message of Ch'an were members of the *Bhikṣu Saṅgha,* the ancient monastic order established by Sākyamuni Buddha, the founder of the Buddhist religion. Following Buddha's noble example great number of men and women left "the dust of the world" and, in accordance with the ancient monastic ideals of purity, poverty, and simplicity, led austere lives dedicated to the pursuit of higher wisdom inherent in the human heart. The monastic character of the Indian tradition was successfully transmitted to China where the Saṅgha performed the same role of upholding and preserving the teaching, and transmitting it to later generations. The lives of the monks were in large part regulated by the Vinaya, the monastic precepts that both protect the monks from coming in contact with situations not conducive to practice, and at the same time reinforce positive physical and mental habits that are helpful for developing clarity and wisdom. Chinese monks received the Vinaya of the Dharmagupta school,[62] and the study and observation of Vinaya were considered essential aspects of the Path by all Chinese schools of Buddhism.

There is not much first-hand information about the monastic life as practiced in the Ch'an monasteries in the eighth and ninth century China. Many of the Ch'an stories provide limited amount of information, albeit in an indirect and restricted way. The oldest description of Ch'an monastic life is a short work entitled *Ch'an-men kuei-shih (Regulations of the Ch'an School)*, which appears in the *Transmission of the Lamp,*[63] compiled by Tao-yüan in 1004. This short text which follows Pai-chang's biographical entry gives an outline of the structure and life in the Ch'an communities during the T'ang. According to this text, in what was by that time a well-established tradition, it was Pai-chang who first established the rules for Ch'an monasteries which came to be widely accepted by all members of the Ch'an school. While from a historical perspective we can trace the beginnings of "Ch'an monasticism"—if we insist on postulating such a thing at all—in the communities on Tung-shan where Tao-hsin and Hung-jen had quite sizeable monastic establishments, it might well be the case that it was during the time of Pai-chang that Ch'an monks came to view their communities as being in some ways distinct from the mainstream of Chinese Buddhism.

> The Master (i.e. Pai-chang) said, "Our school does not belong to either Mahāyāna or Hīnayāna. Neither does it differ from Mahāyāna and Hīnayāna. We should carefully consider them both and establish a rule that will include them both in a harmonious way, and at the same time be appropriate to the needs of the situation." With this in mind, the Master initiated the establishment of separate Ch'an communities.

As can be seen from the above passage, the rules of the Ch'an school took into consideration the traditional monastic practices: both Mahāyāna and Hīnayāna. However, due to the different social circumstances of T'ang China, as well as the particular needs of the monasteries of the new school, the Ch'an masters took an eclectic attitude and tried to adapt the Vinaya without losing its spirit. Nevertheless, the new rules and practices that were developed by the Ch'an masters of T'ang were intended to supplement the Vinaya, not to replace it. From various stories scattered through the records of the school, a picture emerges of many traditional monastic practices—like not eating after noon, keeping the summer retreat *(varṣa),* maintaining strict discipline of body and speech, using formal forms of address, respecting seniority, etc.—being the basic standards for Ch'an monks. There are even recorded efforts to upkeep traditional monastic practices that were not so common among the Chinese Buddhists of the time, like going for alms. One of the deviations from the Vinaya rules were the agricultural activities performed by some Ch'an monks. The Vinaya prohibits monks to engage in farming, and this minor rule seems to have been ignored in the Ch'an communities. Unlike other schools, manual labor came to occupy its own place in Ch'an monastic life, taking on a new spiritual dimension, and becoming an integral part of daily practice. It is difficult to establish the extent of monks' participation in agricultural activities, but there seems to be some exaggeration about it. Many Ch'an masters resided in public monasteries, or started to teach at the invitation of high government officials who were traditionally very generous patrons of monasteries, and it is very unlikely that, with the generous contributions from them and from the general populace, the monks had to exclusively rely on their own labor for their sustenance.[64]

> The monastery should not have a Buddha hall; instead only a Dharma hall should be erected. This is to

symbolize the respect for the transmission from the Buddhas and the patriarchs down to the present age. Those monks who have come to pursue the study should, irrespective of their numbers and social standing, all enter the Saṅgha hall. They should be given a place according to the number of summer retreats since their ordination.[65] Long [sleeping and meditation] platforms should be set up and everyone should be provided with a stand on which to hang his requisites.[66] During rest-time monks should place their pillows on the edge of the platform and lie down on their right flank in the auspicious posture.[67] They should only take a little rest after the long meditation periods, thus maintaining the four dignities of monks-hood at all times.[68]

Except for going to the abbot's quarters to receive personal instructions,[69] the monks should decide by themselves about the amount of effort they put into their practice, and they should not be bound by any rules in this regard.

All the monks in the monastery should attend the morning meditation[70] and the evening meeting. When the Elder (i.e. the abbot) enters the [Dharma] hall and ascends to the high seat to preside over the meeting, all the monks should stand on the sides in files and listen [attentively to what is said]. At that time the monks can raise questions about the essentials of the teaching and engage in an open and alive dialogue with the Elder, so that it is shown how to abide in accord with Dharma.

The two meals of gruel and vegetarian food are shared equally by all.[71] The emphasis on frugality should demonstrate how both the Dharma and the food are to be used.

For the practice of physical labor all monks should be divided into ten groups according to their

> abilities, and each group should have one monk who will serve as a supervisor, making sure that everyone performs his task.

The descriptions in the text suggest that monastic life was a life of renunciation which had its foundation on strict discipline and required full participation from the monks. Though the monks had considerable freedom to use their free time as it seemed fit to them, the freedom was always found within the form which they were expected to follow all the time. In case an insincere individual tried to take an advantage of the situation, when uncovered, he was to be treated harshly.

> If there is someone who falsely pretends [to be a monk], and like a thief enters the pure assembly causing all kinds of disturbance, he should be reported to the Karmadāna[72] who should remove his belongings from his place and expel him from the monastery. This is done out of consideration for the pure assembly. If a monk has committed a [major] offence, then he should be beaten with a stick and his robes, bowl, and other requisites should be burned in front of the community. Then he should be expelled through the side door as a sign of disgrace.

Besides practicing together with other monks in a monastery, the monks undertook pilgrimages during which they would visit holy mountains or call on various masters, with whom they could try to settle their doubts; if they found they could learn more with a particular master, they were welcome to stay with him for any amount of time they wished. Another option for the monks was to live a more hermetic life, where they could deepen their practice in the solitude of the mountains among a natural scenery far away from the dusty world, enjoying the company of the moon and the clouds. This kind of solitary practice was normally undertaken by monks on a higher stage of mental development who had spent many years studying with various teachers, as can be seen from the examples of the monks translated in this volume. The monks enjoyed great freedom to travel and to study with various teachers, and it is largely due to this support of the monastic form which served as a vehicle for transmission of the teaching that the Ch'an school had a period of such extraordinary activity during the T'ang, which enabled many people to cut through their delusions and perceive their real nature. Instead of looking at Ch'an monasticism as a new form of Buddhist monasticism, it might be more appropriate to look at it, with its strict emphasis on sincere practice and strong reliance on the spirit of the teaching, as a return to the original way of the early Indian monks, who like their Chinese brothers led an unattached mendicant lives traveling through the land and meeting teachers in search of the profound mystery.

It is only with this understanding of the monastic context in which the teachings were given that we can start to appreciate the true meaning of the statements of the masters. The lack of emphasis on the foundations of Buddhist practice, especially the strong ethical foundation, does not mean that they are not part of Ch'an practice; on the contrary, they are such an essential aspect of it, that without them one cannot even get started, let alone gain any deeper understanding of Ch'an. The unity of the precepts, the teaching, and Ch'an is explicitly stated by Ma-tsu's disciple Wei-k'uan.

> When the unsurpassed *bodhi* is expressed through the body, it is called Vinaya; when it is expressed through the mouth as speech, it is called Dharma; when it is practiced with the mind, it is Ch'an. Though these are three different functions, they all return to a single reality. It is like different rivers and lakes which have their own names: though the names differ, the

> water's nature is always same. Vinaya is Dharma, and Dharma is not asunder from Ch'an. How could one falsely create any distinctions among the three?[73]

The view that immoral behavior, drinking, improper sexual relationships, desire for control over other people, and the other similar "human weaknesses" can be manifest in the life of someone who has gained deeper insight into the Dharma is unknown in Chinese Buddhism, and certainly has nothing to do with Ch'an. Of course, there have been impostors who, after experiencing some subjective mental states, have in their self-delusion claimed realization, and very often without the noblest of intentions have led others in the same direction. The Ch'an masters have often tried to expose the possible deviations from the Path, and have offered clear guidelines as to what constitutes genuine practice and realization, as well as what are the various forms of self-deception. The earliest treatise that deals with mistaken notions of Ch'an practice is *Kuei-shan ching-ts'e (Kuei-shan's Admonitions)*,[74] written by Kuei-shan, where he emphasizes the importance of self-control and strict keeping of the precepts which according to him are indispensable prerequisites for any aspiring Ch'an practitioner. The same theme was taken again by Fa-yen in the tenth century, and it occurs frequently in the writings of the Sung Dynasty Ch'an masters. The importance of the monastic form and a strong foundation in *śīla* were also emphasized by Chinul (1158-1210), who during the Koryo Dynasty (937-1392) revitalized the Ch'an school in Korea; and by Dōgen (1200-1252), who transmitted the teachings of the Ts'ao-tung lineage to Japan.

## *Tsung-mi's Evaluation of the Hung-chou School*

One of the most valuable sources of information about Ch'an Buddhism during the eighth century are the writings of Kuei-feng Tsung-mi.[75] Besides providing description of the various approaches to Ch'an practice during that time, Tsung-mi also tried to build a bridge between the Ch'an tradition and the scriptures by identifying the approaches of the various schools of Ch'an with the corresponding schools in the scriptural traditions. Being recognized as both a Ch'an master and the fifth patriarch of the Hua-yen school, Tsung-mi was probably the most qualified person to try to draw such parallels; his writings reveal his profound insight into Ch'an and his deep understanding of the teaching of the scriptures.

According to Tsung-mi, the school of Ma-tsu—which he calls Hung-chou school from the name of the area where Ma-tsu, Pai-chang, and other masters of the school had their monasteries—teaches kataphatic approach towards the Dharma, regarding everything as being the Way and being ultimately true. It considers all things as being manifestations of the Buddha-nature, and its practice consists in letting the mind function freely.

> The school [that teaches] direct disclosure of the mind's nature states that all dharmas, whether existent or empty, are nothing but the true nature.[76] The true nature is devoid of characteristics and is inactive. Its essence cannot be described in any way: it is neither profane nor holy, neither cause nor effect, neither good nor evil. However, through its functioning the essence can manifest in numerous ways; it can manifest as profane or holy, with form and appearance. . . . This very thing that is capable of speech and physical activity, of desire, anger, compassion and patience, capable of giving rise to good and evil, and experiencing suffering and joy is precisely your Buddha-nature. This is the original Buddha, and outside of it there is no other Buddha. Because of the spontaneous nature of this fundamental reality it is impossible to arouse the mind to cultivate the Way. The Way

> is mind, and mind cannot be cultivated with mind; evil is also mind, and mind cannot be extinguished by mind. Neither extinguishing nor cultivating, just being oneself and acting in a natural way, that is liberation. The nature is like empty space; it neither increases nor decreases. What use there is in trying to make it complete? Just at all times and all places stop creating any karma, thus nourishing the spirit and supporting the womb of sagehood, spontaneously manifest spiritual wonders. This is true enlightenment, true cultivation, and true attainment.[77]

However, this sole emphasis on the dynamic aspects of the Buddha-nature tends to overlook the absolute immutable nature of its essence. While the True Mind manifests itself through its function which responds to conditions, it is also possessed of inherent function which is overlooked by the Hung-chou school.

> The original essence of the True Mind has two kinds of function: the inherent function of the self-nature, and the function in response to conditions. These can be compared to a bronze mirror. The substance of the bronze represents the essence of the self-nature; the brightness of the bronze represents the function of the self-nature. The images that appear due to the brightness are the function in response to conditions. While there can be numerous images that appear when certain conditions are present, the brightness itself is always bright. The brightness has a single taste which can be taken as a simile for the eternal quiescence of the mind, that is the essence of the self-nature. The constant awareness of the mind is the function of the self-nature, and its ability for speech, discrimination, motion, and so on are its function in response to conditions. So, when the Hung-chou

> [school] points to the ability for speech and the like, that is only the function in response to conditions; they neglect the [inherent] function of the self-nature.[78]

Because of Hung-chou school's claim that "the mind-essence cannot be pointed out; it is only through its ability to manifest through speech and the like that we can verify its existence and realize the Buddha-nature,"[79] Tsung-mi perceives a flaw in its approach. While it is true that both the essence and the function are different aspects of the same reality, at the same time they do differ from each other from the point of conventional reality. This failure to perceive their mutual difference, and instead to reduce the essence to its function, have certain implications for the Hung-chou school's understanding of practice and awakening.

> Now, the Hung-chou school says that greed and anger, *śīla* and *samādhi* are all Buddha-nature. In their emphasis on function, they fail to distinguish between ignorance and enlightenment. Their meaning is that the suchness of the mind-nature is always aware, like the moist nature of water that never changes. Since the mind is free from ignorance, there is no true ignorance. Like a wind that suddenly stops, after awakening all delusions gradually cease like the gradual abating of the waves. The mind and the body become suffused with *samādhi* and wisdom, and one is gradually liberated. . . . The Hung-chou school constantly proposes that since greed, anger, kindness, and virtue are all Buddha- nature, how could there be any difference between them? This is like someone who only perceives the moist nature of water as unchanging, but fails to comprehend that there is a big difference between a boat which crosses the water and one that sinks on the way. Therefore, although this school is

> close to sudden awakening, it does not reach it; as to gradual cultivation, it is altogether mistaken.[80]

While from the point of ultimate reality it is possible to say that all things are manifestations of the True Mind and that ignorance and enlightenment arise from the same source and are ultimately equal, from the point of conventional reality there is conspicuous difference between ignorance and enlightenment, good and evil, and the law of karma is indisputably valid. Within the perfect teaching these two aspects of the one true reality, the ultimate and the conventional, are equally present and mutually interpenetrate in harmonious and unobstructed way. Holding to only one aspect and observing phenomena from its particular perspective only creates a biased view that prevents one from perceiving the ground of harmonious wholeness where all contradictions cease in the light of perfect understanding. It is the tension created by the apparent contradiction between the original enlightenment and universal liberation, and the obvious imperfection and suffering which we all experience, between the understanding that there is nothing to be cultivated and the need for sincere cultivation, that creates the ongoing inspiration and serves as an activating force in the course of Ch'an practice. In Tsung-mi's view, the main shortcoming in the teaching of the Hung-chou school comes from its exclusive emphasis on the ultimate reality, from which they develop one-sided understanding which overlooks conventional reality, thus failing to perceive the differences within unity. Because of this they are unable to see the importance of gradual cultivation and application of effort, and are thus stuck in their partial understanding.

We cannot be sure whether the criticisms mentioned above are directed towards Ma-tsu himself or towards some of his unenlightened followers who made erroneous interpretations of his teaching.[81] There are numerous passages in the records of the masters of the Hung-chou school that leave themselves open to such criticism, but there are also passages in which the Hung-chou school's masters unmistakably point to possible misinterpretations of the Ch'an teaching in very much the same way as Tsung-mi. We might assume that many people did take some of the utterances of the masters of the Hung-chou school out of their context, and applied them to their practice in a way that prompted criticism by more erudite and perceptive monks like Tsung-mi. Indeed, much of the writings of the late T'ang and Sung Ch'an masters are concerned with uncovering wrong approaches to Ch'an practice, and there are frequent complains by the masters of the difficulty in finding someone who truly understands Ch'an. Whosoever might have been the object of Tsung-mi's criticisms, they can certainly be used as helpful pointers by all those who try to understand Ch'an and to use it as a vehicle for spiritual liberation. While the (apparent) radical non-dualism of "everything is the Way" and "there are no defilements to be eradicated" may sound as an attractive theory, or even as the most logical ultimate development of Buddhadharma, taken by itself it does offer very little help in dealing with one's emotional instability and neurotic thought-patterns, and can very easily lend itself to antinomian interpretations which can only serve to perpetuate one's self-deceptions. There have been numerous examples of this, for many of which one does not have to go back in history, which make the writings like those of Tsung-mi even more valuable for the present-day students.

## *A Note on the Translations*

The *Record of Ma-tsu* (*Chiang-hsi ma-tsu tao-i ch'an-shih yu-lu*) on which is based the translation presented in this volume has been compiled during the Ming Dynasty (1368-1644), over a half millennium after Ma-tsu's lifetime. While much of the material can be found in earlier Ch'an collections, most notably the *Ching-te ch'uan-teng lu*, the *Ku tsun-*

*su yü-lu*, and to a smaller extend the *Tsu-t'ang chi*, that still leaves a gap of nearly two centuries between the earliest extant records and the actual events they are said to portray. That gives rise to certain questions. First, how authentic are the materials at our disposal? Do they relate the details about Ma-tsu's life and his teachings accurately? Or are they mere products of late T'ang and early Sung hagiography? In case the authenticity of the materials in question is accepted, how well and how completely do they represent Ma-tsu's teaching?

An attempt to answer these questions in a more thorough way will lead one to a number of related topics about the history and doctrine of Ch'an Buddhism. That will involve critical historical analysis of the period in question, an examination of the relation between T'ang and Sung Dynasty Ch'an, the problem of retributive attribution in Ch'an, etc.. All of this is obviously well beyond the scope of this Introduction. Nonetheless, few brief observation about the issues raised above might be useful for our present purpose.

Concerning the authenticity of the materials which record Ma-tsu's teachings (and the same applies to the materials which concern some of the other masters presented in this volume), the diversity of materials found in the various extant sources along with the different versions of some of Ma-tsu's dialogues suggest that by the second half of the tenth century there have been a number of stories about Ma-tsu's exchanges with his disciples. Some of those stories have either already presented variant accounts of the exchanges, or have been edited, and sometimes considerably altered by the editors of the classical collections which were compiled during that and the subsequent periods. A pertinent example of this is the dialogue between Ma-tsu and Wu-yeh.[82] The short version presented in the *Record* portrays Wu-yeh as been enlightened by Ma-tsu in a very direct and immediate way without resort to any instructions or verbal explanations, very much in harmony with the Sung image about the distinctive methods of the "sudden" school. However, the supposedly earlier version from *Sung kao-seng chuan* contains doctrinal explanations by Ma-tsu—complete with sūtra quotations, quite worthy of a Dharma master!—and portrays Wu-yeh as equally prone to verbosity, and to a certain extend reveals the intellectual content of his realization. Besides these two somewhat contrasting versions, in *Tsu-tang chi* there is a third version of the dialogue, closer to the one found in the *Record*. Whether certain editors have added some extra material to the original(s), or have subtracted certain material to bring the story closer to their ideas about Ma-tsu's teaching style is something we can only guess about. However, it is certain that some (or all) versions of the story do not factually portray the event of Wu-yeh's supposed awakening. (If there is at all a way to adequately convey an exchange of that kind through the medium of letters.)

The structure of the sermons (which comprise the second part of this volume's translation of the *Record*) also casts certain doubts whether they are actual records of talks Ma-tsu has given to his disciples. The texts tend to be somewhat incoherent, often with awkward transitions between paragraphs and abrupt changes of topics which frequently appear to be quite unrelated, all of which is suggestive of somewhat clumsy editing. The materials presented are probably taken from Ma-tsu's teachings, but there is a possibility that the "sermons" might not be records of actual talks Ma-tsu has given. It is possible, but by no means certain, that unknown editors have selected extracts from Ma-tsu's talks and shorter addresses and have put them together with the idea of presenting them in a form which will be representative of Ma-tsu's teaching.

If we take that the bulk of the material from the *Record* does represent actual teachings of Ma-tsu, it might be relevant to consider how representative is that material of the whole of Ma-tsu's teaching, and how helpful it is for reconstructing his thought. According to the *Tsu-tang chi*

Ma-tsu thought for over forty years, while all we now have are just few pages. With such a scarcity of material, as well as the length of time passed since Ma-tsu's lifetime, it seems rather farfetched to propose definitive arguments about Ma-tsu's understanding of Buddhadharma and the ways he tried to convey that understanding to others. That obviously does not mean that we cannot, or should not try to gain better understanding about it.

When studying the texts which are said to contain the teachings of the Hung-chou masters it is useful to distinguish between the different kinds of texts. Roughly, the texts can be classified in three categories: (1) texts written by Hung-chou masters, of which there are only few; (2) sermons recorded by their disciples; and (3) dialogues, i.e. *kung-ans*. The penchant to emphasize only one of this kinds of texts as representative of the tradition—which is often done for the dialogues—does have weighty consequences for one's understanding of the tradition. For example, *Kuei-shan ching-ts'e* with its strong moralistic undertone provides very different reading then some of the stories which depict seemingly somewhat erratic behavior and utterances, to which one can easily impute any meaning and significance. It seems credible to question if the role of the dialogues as a new literary form marking a new Buddhist movement has not been somewhat exaggerated. Is it possible to consider that perhaps they gained the importance typicaly attached to them as a result of a gradual drive in the later Ch'an movement to construe a distinct identity for itself? Perhaps, after all, it might be that the real degradation of Ch'an Buddhism in China did not take place because it got "diluted" by the teachings of the other schools. Perhaps the real decay set in when instead of relying on the sūtras as the source of final authority, the monks' subjects of study consisted of ancient stories which readily lend themselves to any interpretations one wishes to assign to them, without teachers like Ma-tsu to point out the difference between mistaken ideas and genuine realization.

To gain a more adequate understanding of Ma-tsu's teaching, besides careful study of the materials that deal directly with Ma-tsu and the records of his immediate disciples, it is also essential to consider the teachings with which Ma-tsu was familiar, both those which directly shaped his understanding of the Buddhadharma, as well as those which posed the challenge of creative response to their perceived shortcomings. That will include both the Ch'an masters and other eminent monks prior to Ma-tsu, his contemporaries, and most importantly the Mahāyāna sūtras with which he was familiar and which he seems to have used extensively both for his own edification as well as for the purpose of instructing others. As it has been already emphasized, one also has to carefully consider the historical, social, and religious background which certainly influenced his thought and expression. Buddhist movements and their doctrines are not created in a vacuum; (ideally) they are creative responses to changing spiritual needs and social circumstances, and at the same time they represent efforts to return back to the source of the Buddhist religious experience—the Buddha's enlightenment—and the actual ways that experience have been formulated—the teachings of the lineage of enlightened teachers which starts with the historical Buddha.

Most importantly, in order to gain more comprehensive understanding of any Buddhist teachings, they ultimately have to be approached on their own terms. That obviously means undertaking practice by oneself. (Which, contrary to widespread present-day notions, means more then mere engagement in certain "spiritual" exercises motivated by intellectual curiosity, immature yearning for some vague spiritual realm, or penchant for the exotic, not to mention seeking of worldly profit). As it is stated in the *Avataṃsaka Sūtra*:

> Like a person who counts the treasures of others,
> Without himself having half a coin,
> So are the learned ones
> Who do not practice the Dharma.[83]

When approached with the right attitude, the study of the texts which contain the teachings of the ancient Ch'an masters unavoidably points to the one who is undertaking the study. Learning about the ancients is, really, a way to learn about oneself. That is what truly matters.

**NOTES:**

1. See Neal Donner, "Sudden and Gradual intimately Conjoined: Chih-i's T'ien-t'ai View," in Peter N. Gregory, ed., ***Sudden and Gradual: Approaches to Enlightenment in Chinese Thought,*** Studies in East Asian Buddhism, no. 5 (Honolulu: University of Hawaii Press, 1987), p. 201-226.

2. T 278 and T 279, translated by Buddhabhadra (359-429) and Śikṣānanda (652-710) respectively. English translation by Thomas Cleary, *The Flower Ornament Scripture,* 3 vols. (Boston & London: Shambhala Publications, 1984-1987).

3. The term "school" as used here does not denote a special sect or denomination with its own centralized institutional structure. It might be better understood as, to borrow Theodore Foulk's phrase, a "school of thought" which is distinguishable from other "schools" by its adherence to its own set of doctrines and practices, but lacks independent institutional structure. It is a very flexible designation, and besides the compliance to common forms of religious practice, the teachings of various schools greatly overlap and complement each other. The Ch'an school in China never set itself apart from the rest of the *saṅgha* in China. As a matter of fact, the followers of much of what is labeled as Ch'an school by contemporary scholars and Buddhist practitioners never considered themselves as Ch'an Buddhists. Much of the present confusion about Ch'an Buddhism is a result of the fact that much of the information about this religious movement has been derived, or greatly influenced by the interpretations of the Japanese Zen schools which claim to be inheritors of the Ch'an tradition, or by scholars who are prejudiced by the views of the same schools. Some of the Ch'an school's followers did set themselves as a separate sect, or institution, during the Kamakura period *in Japan,* but it is very unlikely that anything of that sort ever existed in China. Of course, there are traces of sectarian biases in Ch'an works, but they are always upheld by people on the periphery of the tradition, not by the great

Ch'an masters themselves. For the place of the Ch'an tradition in the context of Buddhist monasticism, see Theodore Griffit Foulk, "The Ch'an School and its Place in the Buddhist Monastic Tradition" (Ph.D. diss., University of Michigan, Ann Arbor, 1987).

4. Emperor Wu of Liang Dynasty was one of the greatest supporters of Buddhism in Chinese history. The story of his meeting with Bodhidharma forms case 1 of the *Blue Cliff Record.*

5. This is the oldest of the extant three Chinese translations of the sūtra, done in 443 during the (Early) Sung Dynasty (420-479). It is in four *chüan* and there are numerous commentaries on it.

6. When using the designation "patriarch" in reference to these monks, it is important to keep in mind that neither they nor any of the other great masters of later times considered themselves as such. The whole theory of patriarchal transmission was formulated much later by monks of sectarian predilections, during the time when the Ch'an school, or at least some of its followers, started to feel self-conscious of its separate identity. All of the great masters were simply monks who with deep faith engaged in the practice of the religion of the Blessed One, and through their sincere effort they gained realization into the nature of reality, from which out of compassion for other beings, who due to their delusion were creating various kinds of suffering for themselves and others, they, in the best Bodhisattva tradition, came out and made the teaching available to those who wished to use it.

7. David W. Chappell, "The Teachings of the Fourth Patriarch Tao-hsin (580-658)," in Lai and Lancaster, eds. *Early Ch'an in China and Tibet*. Berkeley Buddhist Studies Series, no.5 (Berkeley: Asian Humanities Press, 1983), p. 89-91.

8. This important document belongs to the group of texts that were discovered at the beginning of this century in the caves of Tun-huang in western China. Compiled by Ching-chüeh, it contains a history of the Ch'an school till the middle of the eight century. It considers Gunabhadra, the translator of the *Laṅkāvatāra Sūtra,* as the first patriarch, and it reckons Shen-hsiu as the seventh. It is possible that this text was responsible for the tradition that considered the *Laṅkāvatāra Sūtra* as the main sūtra transmitted by the Ch'an patriarchs. For an English translation of this text, see J. C. Cleary, *Zen Dawn: Early Zen Texts from Tun Huang* (Boston: Shambhala Publications, 1986), p. 19-78.

9. This early Ch'an document has been lost and the only

information about its contents comes from *Leng-ch'ieh shih-tzu chi,* which quotes from it. Its compiler, Hsüan-tse, was one of Hung-jen's disciples and was the teacher of Ching-chüeh, the author of *Leng-ch'ieh shih-tzu chi.* See Philip B. Yampolski, *The Platform Sūtra of the Sixth Patriarch* (New York: Columbia University Press, 1967), p. 16-18.

10. English translation in John R. McRae, *The Northern School and the Formation of Early Ch'an Buddhism,* Studies in East Asian Buddhism, no. 3 (Honolulu: University of Hawaii Press, 1986), p. 121-132.

11. Ibid. p. 136-137.

12. For a comprehensive study of Shen-hsiu's life and thought and the history of the Northern school of Ch'an see John R. McRae's *The Northern School and the Formation of Early Ch'an Buddhism.* I am indebted to McRae's work for this part of the Introduction.

13. Detailed analysis of the history and contents of the *Platform Sutra,* and the life of Hui-neng can be found in Yampolsky's *The Platform Sūtra of the Sixth Patriarch.*

14. This monastery is located in Kwangchow, the capital of Kwangtung Province. Its present name is Kuang-hsiao Monastery.

15. According to one account Shih-t'ou became a monk with the Sixth Patriarch Hui-neng at the age of thirteen. After the death of the Sixth Patriarch he went to study with his disciple Hsing-ssu. In 742 he arrived at Nan-yüeh, where he built himself a grass hut on a big flat rock and entered a period of solitary practice. In 764 he accepted the invitation from a group of Ch'an students to came out of seclusion and start to teach. He had many disciples, among whom the most famous were Yao-shan Wei- yen, Tan-hsia T'ien-jan, and Tao-wu Yüan-chih.

16. See John McRae, "The Ox-head School of Chinese Ch'an Buddhism: From early Ch'an to the Golden Age," in Robert M. Gimello and Peter Gregory, eds. *Studies in Ch'an and Hua Yen,* Studies in East Asian Buddhism, no. 1. (Honolulu: University of Hawaii Press, 1983), p. 195.

17. T 2075. vol. 51, p. 179a-196b. For more information about this treatise and Ch'an in Szechwan see Yanagida Seizan, "The *Li-tai fa-pao chi* and the Ch'an Doctrine of Sudden Awakening," translated by Carl W. Bielefeldt, in Whalen Lai and Lewis Lancaster, eds. *Early Ch'an in China and Tibet,* Berkeley Buddhist

Series, no.5. (Berkeley: Asian Humanities Press, 1983), p. 13-49.

18. Tsung-mi regards the schools of Wu-hsiang and Wu-chu as separate schools. From Tsung-mi's account it appears that the school of Wu-chu, which he calls the Pao-t'ang school, carried the doctrine of no-thought to its ultimate conclusion, which led it to deny the validity of any ethical observances and traditional practices.

19. See *Yüan-chüeh ching ta-shu ch'ao,* HTC vol. 14, p. 279c. English translation in Jan Yun-hua, "Tsung-mi: His Analysis of Ch'an Buddhism," *T'oung Pao* 58 (Leiden, 1972), p. 48-49.

20. The same is valid for the other school of Chinese Buddhism from the Sui-T'ang period. For example, the T'ien-t'ai school did not exist during the lifetime of its "founder" Chih-i, and there was nothing closely resembling any "Hua-yen school" at the time of the Hua-yen "patriarchs."

21. The Fa-yen school, the last of the five Ch'an schools that were formed during the late T'ang and the Five Dynasties period.

22. *Tsung-men shih-kuei lun*, HTC vol. 110, p. 439a-b.

23. For the question of the authenticity of the materials about Ma-tsu see the last chapter of the Introduction. Here I merely relate the bare outline of his life according to the extant materials, and try to avoid redundant speculations, unless there is a reasonably reliable basis for them in the oldest texts.

24. HTC vol. 14, p. 279a. English translation of the relevant passages in Jan, p. 45-47.

25. According to Tsung-mi the third phrase was later changed by Wu-chu to "no-falsehood" (*mo-wang*). Wu-chu thought that the disciples of Wu-hsiang have misunderstood their teacher. See HTC vol 14, p. 278d.

26. Yanagida, p. 29-30.

27. HTC vol. 14, p. 278b-c; cf. Jan, p. 43.

28. The year of his ordination can be inferred from the information given in his entry in *Sung kao-seng chuan (Sung Biographies of Eminent Monks)* which states that he spent fifty years as a monk, which leads us to the year of 738.

29. A possible link between Ma-tsu and the Northern School has been suggested by McRae in his *The Northern School*, p. 93-94. The evidence which he introduces, however, is inadequate at best.

30. Ibid. p. 90-91.

31. See HTC vol. 14, p. 279a; also see Jan, p. 45-46.

32. Prajñātāra is the putative twenty-seventh patriarch of the Ch'an school. A native of eastern India, he was the teacher of Bodhidharma.

33. CTL *chüan* 5, Huai-jang's entry.

34. If we accept the statement in the *Tsu-tang chi* that Ma-tsu taught for over forty years, that would imply that he left Huai-jang before 750 and immediately started to teach.

35. K'ai-yüan Monastery belonged to a network of state-supported monasteries which was established in 738 by the Emperor Hsüan-tsung (r. 712-750). See Stanley Weinstein, *Buddhism under the T'ang* (Cambridge: Cambridge University Press, 1987), p. 53-54.

36. Or eighty-eight according to the *Tsu-tang chi*. It seems that further a text is removed from Ma-tsu's lifetime, the greater is the number of his close disciples it cites.

37. *Sung kao-seng chuan,* T 2061. vol. 50, p. 764a.

38. T 2015. vol. 48, p. 404b-c. Cf. Jeffrey Lyle Broughton, "Kuei-feng Tsung-mi: The Convergence of the Ch'an and the Teachings" (Ph.D. diss., Columbia University, 1975), p. 188-189.

39. Huang-po Tuan-chi, *Ch'uan hsin fa-yao* (Taipei: Fo-chiao ch'u-pan she, 1984), p. 2.

40. T 2016. vol. 48, p. 492a.

41. HTC vol. 118, p. 87b.

42. See the beginning of the second sermon in the *Record of Ma-tsu* in this volume.

43. CTL *chüan* 10, Chao-chou's entry. This dialogue is case no. 19 in *Wu-men kuan* (*Wu-men's Barrier*).

44. See note 46 on the *Record of Ma-tsu.*

45. See the end of the second sermon in this volume's translation of the *Record of Ma-tsu.*

46. See the end of the third sermon.

47. HTC vol. 118, p. 85a.

48. CTL *chüan* 9, Kuei-shan's entry.

49. Vimalakīrti is the hero of the *Vimalakīrti Sūtra*. A fabulous character, he is described as a rich layman whose understanding of Dharma surpasses that of the rest of the Buddha's disciples, with the exception of Mañjuśrī. He represents the principle of being in the world, but not of the world. The *Vimalakīrti Sūtra* is one of

the sūtras which were held in high esteem in Ch'an circles, and is the sūtra most often quoted in the *Record of Ma-tsu*.

50. Bodhisattva Fu (Fu Ta-shih) is one of the most famous laymen in Chinese Buddhism. He lived during the reign of Emperor Wu of Liang Dynasty, and was highly respected by the Emperor who often sought his instructions and advice. He is often mentioned in Ch'an texts.

51. The literal meaning is to receive the *Saṅgha*'s assent at its meeting (*jñapticaturtha-karman)*. It refers to the monastic practice of requesting the community's agreement on certain issues, like confession or ordination, by making announcement and then passing a motion three times.

52. HTC vol. 118, p. 82d.

53. See Kuei-shan ching-ts'e, HTC vol. 111, p. 147b. Also see Melvin M. Takemoto, "Kuei-shan ching-ts'e: Morality and the Hung-chou School of Ch'an" (M.A. thesis, University of Hawaii, 1983), p. 87.

54. See note 21 on the *Record.*

55. "Appearance of the *Tathāgata*" chapter, *Avataṃsaka Sūtra*. Cf. Thomas Cleary, *The Flower Ornament Scripture*, vol. 2 (Boston & London: Shambhala Publications, 1986), p. 315.

56. "Eulogies in the Palace of Suyāma Heaven" chapter, *Avataṃsaka Sūtra*. Cf. Cleary, vol. 1, p. 452.

57. "Eulogies in the Palace of Tuṣita Heaven" chapter, *Avataṃsaka Sūtra*. Cf. Cleary, vol. 1, p. 528.

58. "Ten Practices" chapter, *Avataṃsaka Sūtra*. Cf. Cleary, vol. 1, p. 465.

59. When the river is crossed, the raft is left behind. Similarly, when the river of *saṃsāra* is crossed with the help of the teaching, one reaches the other shore of Nirvāṇa and can abandon the teaching. As Chuang-tzu puts it, "when the fish is caught, the trap is abandoned."

60. This is by no means to suggest that the practice of Ch'an was solely confined to the monastic community. On the contrary, many of the literati and government officials during the T'ang Dynasty actively pursued Ch'an practice and were frequent visitors to Ch'an monasteries. However, it was considered most natural that all those who decided to completely dedicate themselves to the practice would renounce all worldly concerns and become monks. The nature of the practice and the formidable difficulties involved in it

are such that single-minded dedication is essential for any true attainment, and the monkshood with its clearly defined priorities is greatly supportive in that respect. It is not that the masters attained realization because of being monks, but rather they become monks in order to attain realization, and the monastic form proved to be of great help for that purpose. For a description of lay practice during the T'ang, see the account of the Buddhist practice of Po Chü-i (772-846), one of the greatest poets and literati of the T'ang Dynasty, in Kenneth Ch'en, *The Chinese Transformation of Buddhism* (Princeton: Princeton University Press, 1973), p. 184-339. Po Chü-i is especially pertinent example for our purpose since he studied under number of Ch'an monks, among whom were Ma-tsu's disciple Wei-k'uan and Tsung-mi, both of whom are mentioned in this Introduction.

61. It can also be pointed out that by no means all Ch'an masters of that period displayed penchant for unconventional behavior. As Ven. Yin-shun has perceptively noted, the display of such methods as shouts and blows by individual masters is connected to the area of China where they come from. It seems that masters from the north (e.g. Lin-chi) tend to be more inclined towards "crude" behavior in comparison with the masters from the south (e.g. Kuei-shan). The same pattern is discernable among Shih-t'ou's disciples. Most of them were from the area south of the Yangtze River valley, which may account for the paucity of more drastic unconventional methods in their demonstration of the Dharma. This seems to imply that the iconoclastic elements found among the Ch'an masters of the period are more a reflection of local cultural patterns then an essential factor in their teaching. See Yin-shun, *Chung-kuo ch'an-tsung shih* (Taipei: Cheng-wen ch'u-pan she, 1983), p. 410-414.

62. One of the twenty "Hīnayāna" schools in India. Its *Prātimokṣa* (*Pātimokkha* in Pāli—"Code of Discipline") consists of two-hundred and fifty rules and is very similar to the Theravāda *Pātimokkha*.

63. CTL *chüan* 6. For more detailed studies of this text and its full translation see Martin Collcutt, "The early Ch'an Monastic Rule: *Ch'ing kuei* and the Shaping of Ch'an Community Life," in *Early Ch'an in China and Tibet*, p. 165-184, and Foulk, p. 328-383. I am indebted to these two works for the present translations from this text.

64. Kuei-shan and Huang-po were supported by P'ei-hsiu, the prime minister of China and one of the most noted lay Buddhists of the time; Lin-chi's patron was Wang Ch'ang-shih, the powerful ruler of Hopei province; Ma-tsu resided at the state-supported K'ai-yüan Monastery and had Lu Ssu-kung, the Hung-chou district magistrate, as his disciple. There are also records of lay patrons bringing food to the monastery to offer to the monks.

65. According to the Vinaya regulations, the seniority of a monk is judged from the number of *varṣas* (summer retreats) he has spent as a monk. The more *varṣas* a monk has, greater is his seniority and higher his position in the community, which is reflected in the sitting and sleeping arrangements where he is given precedence over more junior monks.

66. The monks' requisites consist of the set of three robes, bowl, razor, and few personal belonging which may include a book, rosary, cup, etc..

67. This is the reclining posture that Buddha assumed on his entry into *Parinirvāṇa*. He is often depicted in this posture in Buddhist art.

68. The four dignities are dignity in the standing, sitting, walking, and reclining postures, which embrace all activities of daily life.

69. Alternative reading could be "Except for those monks who receive personal instructions from the abbot." This would imply that those monks who through their sincere application of effort have gained the privilège to receive private instructions from the abbot would have greater responsibility to practice, and would be expected to follow certain regime that would not be expected from the rest of the community.

70. Though the term *chao-ts'an* ("morning practice") is taken to mean morning meditation, it is possible that it have started to be used in this sense during the Sung Dynasty, and it might have had different meaning during the T'ang.

71. According to the Vinaya monks can have two meals. The morning meal consists of rice gruel, while the midday meal can include variety of foods, and it should be taken before noon.

72. This is one of the monastic official titles. It is given to a monk who directs the general affairs of the monastery.

73. CTL *chüan* 7, Wei-k'uan's entry.

74. This important text is one of the very few works written by a master of the Hung-chou school of Ch'an. It provides very valuable information about the place of morality in the Ch'an school and about the relationship between Ch'an and traditional Buddhist practices. For the Chinese text and its English translation, see note 53 above.

75. Tsung-mi was born in 780 in Hsi-ch'un province in present-day Szechwan. His family name was Ho, and his family was one of the most wealthy and influential families in the area. During his youth he received traditional Chinese education which included study of the Confucian classics. At the age of twenty-five he decided to become a monk upon meeting a Ch'an monk who greatly impressed him. During the early part of his monastic life as a Ch'an monk Tsung-mi familiarized himself with the teachings of the Southern school of Ch'an. Later on, when he moved to central China, he came in contact with the teachings of the Hua-yen school, an event that signaled a major shift in his religious life. In 812 he met Ch'eng-kuan, the reputed fourth patriarch of the Hua-yen school, and become his disciple. A prolific writer, he is author of a number of commentaries on the sūtras and *śāstras*, as well as a number of works that encompass such varied subjects as Buddhist rituals, the Vinaya, the teachings and history of the Ch'an school, various aspects of the Buddhist doctrine, etc.. The best study of Tsung-mi's life and teaching in English language are the two articles by Jan Yun-hua: "Tsung-mi: His Analysis of Ch'an Buddhism." *T'oung Pao* 58 (Leiden, 1972), p. 1-54, and "Conflict and Harmony in Ch'an Buddhism." *Journal of Chinese Philosophy* 4 (1977), p. 287-302. Also see Jeffrey L. Broughton, "Kuei-feng Tsung-mi: The Convergence of Ch'an and the Teachings" (Ph.D. diss., Columbia University, 1975). Parts of Tsung-mi's writings with comments by the Korean monk Chinul can be found in Robert E. Buswell, *The Korean Approach to Zen: The Collected Works of Chinul* (Honolulu: University of Hawaii Press, 1983), p. 263-374. Peter N. Gregory's comprehensive and well written *Tsung-mi and the Sinification of Chinese Buddhism* (Princeton: Princeton University Press, 1991) unfortunately came out after the manuscript for the present volume was completed, and I was thereby unable to consult any of the excellent material contained in it.

76. Tsung-mi considers both the Hung-chou school and

the Ho-tse school of Shen-hui, to which he belonged, as teaching "direct disclosure of the mind's nature." He identifies this approach to Dharma with the *tathāgatagarbha* doctrine, especially as found in the *Avataṃsaka Sūtra*.

77. *Ch'an-yüan chu-ch'üan-chi tu-hsü*, T 2015. vol. 48, p. 402c. Cf. Jan, p. 39.

78. *Chung-hua ch'uan hsin-ti ch'an-men shih-tzu ch'eng-hsi t'u*, HTC vol. 110, p. 437d. I have adapted the translation from Robert Buswell's *The Korean Approach to Zen*, p. 277.

79. HTC vol. 110, p. 437d.

80. Ibid. p. 438a-b.

81. While in his *Chung-hua ch'üan hsin-ti ch'an-men shih-tzu ch'eng-hsi t'u* Tsung-mi tends to be quite critical of Hung-chou school's approach, in his *Ch'an-yüan chu-ch'üan-chi tu-hsü* he is much more lenient towards it. As a matter of fact, in the second work he equates the teaching of the Hung-chou school, together with Shen-hui's teaching, with the teaching which directly discloses the mind nature—the highest teaching in his taxonomy of the Buddhist teachings.

82. Dialogue 11 in the present translation of the *Record of Ma-tsu*.

83. "Bodhisattva's Request for Illumination" chapter, *Avataṃsaka Sūtra*. Cf. Cleary, vol. 1, p. 306.

## *Part Two*
## *The Record of Ma-tsu*

# *Biography*

Ch'an Master Tao-i of Kiangsi was born in Shih-fang county in Han-chou province.[1] His family name was Ma. He left home [to become a novice monk] at Lo-han Monastery in his home town. His appearance was unusual: he walked with the dignity of a bull, and his stare was like that of a tiger. When he stuck out his tongue, it reached his nose; on his soles there were two wheel marks.[2] In his youth he had his head shaved by Venerable T'ang of Tzu-chou.[3] He received the *bhikṣu* precepts from Vinaya Master Yüan of Yu-chou.[4]

During the K'ai-yüan period of T'ang Dynasty (713-742) he was practicing *samādhi* at Ch'üan-fa Monastery in Heng-yüeh.[5] There he met Venerable Huai-jang,[6] who immediately recognized him as a Dharma-vessel.[7] Huai-jang asked him, "Why are you sitting in meditation?"

The Master replied, "Because I want to become a Buddha." Thereupon Huai-jang took a brick and started to polish it in front of the Master's hermitage. The Master asked him, "Why are you polishing that brick?"

Huai-jang replied, "Because I want to make a mirror."

The Master asked, "How can you make a mirror by polishing a brick?"

Huai-jang said, "If I cannot make a mirror by polishing a brick, how can you become a Buddha by sitting in meditation?"

The Master asked, "Then what shall I do?"

Huai-jang asked, "When an ox-carriage stops moving, do you hit the carriage or the ox?" The Master had no reply. Huai-jang continued, "Are you practicing to sit in meditation, or practicing to sit like a Buddha? As to sitting in meditation, meditation is neither sitting nor lying. As to sitting like a

Buddha, the Buddha has no fixed form. In the non-abiding Dharma, one should neither grasp nor reject. If you try to sit like a Buddha, you are just killing the Buddha. If you attach to the form of sitting, you will never realize the principle."

Upon hearing this the Master felt as if he had tasted ghee.[8] He bowed and asked, "How should one's mind be so that it will accord with the formless *samādhi*?"

Huai-jang said, "Your study of the teaching of the mind-ground is like planting a seed. My teaching of the essentials of the Dharma is like heaven bestowing rain. Because you have natural affinity, you will perceive the Way."

The Master also asked, "The Way is without form; how can it be perceived?"

Huai-jang said, "The Dharma-eye of the mind-ground can perceive the Way. It is same with the formless *samādhi*."

The Master asked, "Is that still subject to becoming and decay?"

Huai-jang said, "If you see the Way trough such concepts as becoming and decay, meeting and parting, then you do not truly see the Way. Listen to my verse:

The mind ground contains various seeds,
Which with rain will come to sprout.
The flower of *samādhi* is formless,
How can it decay or become."

The Master was awakened and his mind became detached. He stayed to serve Huai-jang for ten years, gradually deepening his understanding of the profound mystery.

In the past, the Sixth Patriarch told Venerable Huai-jang: "Patriarch Prajñātāra of India has made a prophecy that from beneath your feet a horse will appear that will stamp to death the people in the world." This referred to the Master.[9]

From among the six disciples of Huai-jang, it was only the Master who secretly received the mind-seal.[10] After that he moved from Fo-chi Ling, a mountain in Chien-yang,[11] to Lin-ch'uan.[12] Later he went to Kung-kung Mountain in

Nan-k'ang.[13] During the Ta-li period (776-779) he settled at K'ai-yüan Monastery in Chung-lin.[14] At that time the provincial governor Lu Ssu-kung heard about Master's reputation, and came to personally receive the teaching from the Master. From then on, students from the four directions gathered around his seat like clouds.

When Huai-jang heard that the Master was teaching in Kiangsi, he asked the monks in his assembly, "Has Tao-i started teaching?"

They told him, "Yes, he has started teaching."

Huai-jang said, "There has been no one to bring any news from there." He then asked one of the monks to go to the Master [and instructed him that] as soon as the Master enters the hall to teach, to ask him, "How is it?" and then to return to report what has happened.

The monk did as he was instructed. When he asked the question, the Master replied, "Since I left confusion behind, for the last thirty years I have been lacking neither salt nor sauce." When the monk returned to Huai-jang and reported what had been said, Huai-jang approved of it.

The Master had one hundred and thirty-nine close disciples, all of whom became teachers in different areas, thus continuing his teaching.[15]

During the first month of the fourth year of the Chen-yüan period (788), the Master climbed Shih-men Mountain in Chien-ch'ang.[16] As he was walking through the forest, he saw a cave which was very flat. He told his attendant, "Next month my old and useless body should return to this place." Having said that, they returned to the monastery.

Not long afterwards the Master become ill. The head monk asked him, "How is the Venerable feeling these days?"

The Master replied, "Sun-Face Buddha, Moon-Face Buddha."[17] On the first day of the second month, after having taken a bath, he sat cross-legged and passed away. During the Yüan-ho period (806-820) he received the posthumous title Ch'an Master Ta-chi (Great Quiescence). The stupa built in his memory was called "Great Adornment."

# *Sermons*

## 1

The Patriarch said to the assembly,[18] "All of you should believe that your mind is Buddha, that this mind is identical with Buddha. The Great Master Bodhidharma came from India to China, and transmitted the One Mind teaching of Mahāyāna so that it can lead you all to awakening. Fearing that you will be too confused and will not believe that this One Mind is inherent in all of you, he used the *Laṅkāvatāra Sūtra* to seal the sentient beings' mind-ground. Therefore, in the *Laṅkāvatāra Sūtra*, mind is the essence of all the Buddha's teachings, no gate is the Dharma-gate.[19]

"'Those who seek the Dharma should not seek for anything.'[20] Outside of mind there is no other Buddha, outside of Buddha there is no other mind. Not attaching to good and not rejecting evil, without reliance on either purity or defilement, one realizes that the nature of offence is empty: it cannot be found in each thought because it is without self-nature. Therefore, the three realms are mind-only and 'all phenomena in the universe are marked by a single Dharma.'[21] Whenever we see form, it is just seeing the mind. The mind does not exist by itself; its existence is due to form. Whatever you are saying, it is just a phenomenon which is identical with the principle. They are all without obstruction and the fruit of the way to '*bodhi* is also like that. Whatever arises in the mind is called form; when one knows all forms to be empty, then birth is identical with no-birth. If one realizes this mind, then one can always wear one's robes and eat one's food. Nourishing the womb of sagehood, one spontaneously passes one's time: what else is there to do? Having received my teaching, listen to my verse:

The mind-ground is always spoken of,
*Bodhi* is also just peace.
When phenomena and the principle are all without obstruction,
The very birth is identical with no-birth."

2

A monk asked, "What is the cultivation of the Way?"

The Patriarch replied, "The Way does not belong to cultivation. If one speaks of any attainment through cultivation, whatever is accomplished in that way is still subject to regress. That is the same as the *Śrāvakas*. If one says that there is no need for cultivation, that is the same as the ordinary people."

The monk also asked, "What kind of understanding should one have in order to comprehend the Way?"

The Patriarch replied, "The self-nature is originally complete. If one only does not get hindered by either good or evil things, then that is a person who cultivates the Way. Grasping good and rejecting evil, contemplating *śūnyatā* and entering *samādhi*—all of these belong to activity. If one seeks outside, one goes away from it. Just put an end to all mental conceptions in the three realms. If there is not a single thought, then one eliminates the root of birth and death and obtains the unexcelled treasury of the Dharma king.

"Since limitless *kalpas*, all worldly false thinking, [such as] flattery, dishonesty, self-esteem, and arrogance have formed one body. That is why the sūtra says, 'It is only through the grouping of many dharmas that this body is formed. When it arises, it is only dharmas arising; when it ceases, it is only dharmas ceasing. When the dharmas arise, they do not say I arise; when they cease, they do not say I cease.'[22]

"'The previous thought, the following thought, and the present thought, each thought does not wait for the others; each thought is calm and extinct.'[23] This is called Ocean Seal *Samādhi*.[24] It contains all dharmas. Like hundreds and thousands of different streams—when they return to the great ocean, they are all called water of the ocean. [The water of the ocean] has one taste which contains all tastes.[25] In the great ocean all streams are mixed together; when one bathes in the ocean, he uses all waters.

"The *Śrāvakas* are awakened, and yet still ignorant; the ordinary people are ignorant about awakening. The *Śrāvakas* do not know that originally the Holy Mind is without any position, without cause and effect, without stages, mental conceptions, and false thoughts. By cultivating causes they attain the fruits and dwell in the *samādhi* of emptiness from twenty to eighty-thousand *kalpas*.[26] Though already awakened, their awakening is the same as ignorance. All Bodhisattvas view this as suffering of the hells: falling into emptiness, abiding in extinction, unable to see the Buddha-nature.

"There might be someone of superior capacity who meets a virtuous friend and receives instructions from him.[27] If upon hearing the words he gains understanding, then without passing through the stages, suddenly he is awakened to the original nature. That is why the sūtra says, 'Ordinary people can still change, but not the *Śrāvakas*.'[28]

"It is in contrast to ignorance that one speaks of awakening. Since originally there is no ignorance, awakening also need not be established. All living beings have since limitless *kalpas* ago been abiding in the *samādhi* of the Dharma-nature. While in the *samādhi* of the Dharma-nature, they wear their clothes, eat their food, talk and respond to things. Making use of the six senses, all activity is the Dharma-nature. It is because of not knowing how to return to the source, that they follow names and seek forms, from which confusing emotions and falsehood arise, thereby creating various kinds of karma. When within a single thought one reflects and illuminates within, then everything is the Holy Mind.

"All of you should penetrate your own minds; do not record my words. Even if principles as numerous as the sands of Ganges are spoken of, the mind does not increase. And if nothing is said, the mind does not decrease. When there is speech, it is just your own mind. If there is silence, it is still your own mind. Even if one could produce various transformation bodies,[29] emit rays of light and manifest the eighteen transmutations,[30] that is still not like becoming like dead ashes.[31]

"Wet ashes are without power, and can be compared to the *Śrāvakas* who falsely cultivate causes in order to obtain the fruits. Dry ashes are with power, and are like the Bodhisattvas whose karma is mature and who are not defiled by any evil. If one is to speak about all expedient teachings of the *tripiṭaka* that the *Tathāgata* has expounded, even after innumerable *kalpas* one still will not be able to finish them all. It is like an endless chain. But if one can awaken to the Holy Mind, then there is nothing else to do. You have been standing long enough. Take care!"

## 3

The Patriarch said to the assembly, "The Way needs no cultivation, just do not defile. What is defilement? When with a mind of birth and death one acts in a contrived way, then everything is defilement. If one wants to know the Way directly: Ordinary Mind is the Way![32] What is meant by Ordinary Mind? No activity, no right or wrong, no grasping or rejecting, neither terminable nor permanent, without worldly or holy. The sūtra says, 'Neither the practice of ordinary people, nor the practice of sages, that is the Bodhisattva's practice.'[33] Just like now, whether walking, standing, sitting, or reclining, responding to situations and dealing with people as they come: everything is the Way. The Way is identical with the *dharmadhātu*. Out of sublime functions as numerous as the sands of Ganges, none of them is outside the *dharmadhātu.* If that was not so, how could it have been said that the mind-ground is a Dharma gate, that it is an inexhaustible lamp.

"All dharmas are mind dharmas; all names are mind names. The myriad dharmas are all born from the mind; the mind is the root of the myriad dharmas. The sūtra says, 'It is because of knowing the mind and penetrating the original source that one is called a *śramaṇa.*' The names are equal, the meanings are equal: all dharmas are equal. They are all pure without mixing. If one attains to this teaching, then one is always free. If the *dharmadhātu* is established, then everything is the *dharmadhātu.* If suchness is established, then everything is suchness. If the principle is established, then all dharmas are the principle. If phenomena are established, then all dharmas are phenomena. When one is raised, thousands follow. The principle and phenomena are not different; everything is wonderful function, and there is no other principle. They all come from the mind.

"For instance, though the reflections of the moon are many, the real moon is only one. Though there are many springs of water, water has only one nature. There are myriad phenomena in the universe, but empty space is only one. There are many principles that are spoken of, but 'unobstructed wisdom is only one.'[34] Whatever is established, it all comes from One Mind. Whether constructing or sweeping away, all is sublime function; all is oneself. There is no place to stand where one leaves the Truth. The very place one stands on is the Truth; it is all one's being. If that was not so, then who is that? All dharmas are Buddhadharmas and all dharmas are liberation. Liberation is identical with suchness: all dharmas never leave suchness. Whether walking, standing, sitting or reclining, everything is always inconceivable function. The sūtras say that the Buddha is everywhere.

"The Buddha is merciful and has wisdom. Knowing well the nature and characters of all beings,[35] he is able to break through the net of beings' doubts. He has left the bondages of existence and nothingness; with all feelings of worldliness and holiness extinguished, [he perceives that] both self and dharmas are empty. He turns the incomparable [Dharma] wheel. Going beyond numbers and measures, his activity is unobstructed and he penetrates both the principle and phenomena.

"Like a cloud in the sky that suddenly appears and then is gone without leaving any traces; also like writing on water, neither born nor perishable: that is the Great Nirvāṇa.

"In bondage it is called *tathāgatagarbha;* when liberated it is called the pure *dharmakāya. Dharmakāya* is boundless, its essence neither increasing nor decreasing. In order to respond to beings, it can manifest as big or small, square or round. It is like a reflection of the moon in water. It functions smoothly without establishing roots.

"'Not obliterating the conditioned; not dwelling in the unconditioned.'[36] The conditioned is the function of the unconditioned; the unconditioned is the essence of the conditioned. Because of not dwelling on support, it has been said, 'Like space which rests on nothing.'[37]

"The mind can be spoken of [in terms of its two aspects]: birth and death, and suchness.[38] The mind as suchness is like a clear mirror which can reflect images. The mirror symbolizes the mind; the images symbolize the dharmas. If the mind grasps at dharmas, then it gets involved in external causes and conditions, which is the meaning of birth and death. If the mind does not grasp at dharmas, that is suchness.

"The *Śrāvakas* hear about the Buddha-nature, while the Bodhisattva's eye perceives the Buddha-nature.[39] The realization of non-duality is called equal nature. Although the nature is free from differentiation, its function is not the same: when ignorant it is called consciousness; when awakened it is called wisdom. Following the principle is awakening, and following phenomena is ignorance. Ignorance is to be ignorant of one's original mind. Awakening is to awake to one's original nature. Once awakened, one is awakened forever, there being no more ignorance. Like, when the sun comes, then all darkness disappears. When the sun of *prajñā* emerges, it does not coexist with the darkness of the defilements. If one comprehends the mind and the objects, then false thinking is not created again. When there is no more false thinking, that is acceptance of the non-arising of all dharmas.[40] Originally it exists and it is present now, irrespective of cultivation of the Way and sitting in meditation. Not cultivating and not sitting is the *Tathāgata*'s pure meditation. If you now truly understand the real meaning of this, then do not create any karma. Content with your lot, pass your life. One bowl, one robe; whether sitting or standing, it is always with you. Keeping *śīla,* you accumulate pure karma. If you can be like this, how can there be any worry that you will not realize? You have been standing long enough. Take care!"

# *Dialogues*

1

Once Hsi-t'ang, Pai-chang, and Nan-ch'üan accompanied the Patriarch to watch the moon. The Patriarch asked, "What shall we do now?"

Hsi-T'ang said, "We should make offerings."

Pai-chang said, "It is best to practice."

Nan-ch'üan shook his sleeves and went away. The Patriarch said, "The sūtras enter the treasury, meditation returns to the sea. It is P'u-yüan alone that goes beyond all things."[41]

2

Once, as Nan-ch'üan was serving gruel to the community of monks, the Patriarch asked him, "What is in the bucket?"

Nan-ch'üan said, "This old man should keep his mouth shut. What is this talk all about?" The Patriarch did not respond.

3

Pai-chang asked, "What is the direction of the Buddhas?"

"It is the very place where you let go of your body and mind." replied the Patriarch.

4

When Ta-chu came to see the Patriarch for the first time, the Patriarch asked him, "Where are you coming from?"

"I am coming from Ta-yün Monastery in Yüeh-chou." replied Ta-chu.

The Patriarch asked him, "What is your intention in coming here?"

Ta-chu said, "I have come here to seek the Buddhadharma."

The Patriarch said, "Without looking at your own treasure, for what purpose are you leaving your home and walking around? Here I do not have a single thing. What Buddhadharma are you looking for?"

Ta-chu bowed, and asked, "What is Hui-hai's own treasure?"[42]

The Patriarch said, "That which is asking me right now is your own treasure—perfectly complete, it lacks nothing. You are free to use it; why are you seeking outside?" Upon hearing this, Ta-chu realized the original mind without relying on knowledge and understanding. Overjoyed, he paid his respects to the Patriarch and thanked him. After this he stayed with him for six years and served him as his disciple.

Later he returned [to Yüeh-chou][43] and composed a treatise entitled *Essentials of Entering the Way Through Sudden Awakening* in one *chüan*. When the Patriarch saw the text, he said to the assembly, "In Yüeh-chou there is a great pearl (*ta-chu*); its perfect brilliance shines freely without obstruction."

5

Ch'an Master Fa-hui of Le-t'an[44] asked the Patriarch, "What is the meaning of 'Patriarch [Bodhidharma's] coming from the West?"

The Patriarch said, "I am going to tell you quietly; come closer." As Fa-hui stepped forward, the Patriarch gave him a blow, saying, "It is not to be discussed in front of another person. Come back tomorrow."

The next day Fa-hui entered the Dharma hall again and asked, "May the Venerable say something, please."

The Patriarch said, "Go and wait till I am about to give a talk; then come out and I will testify to you."

On hearing this Fa-hui had awakening, and said, "Thanks to the great assembly for testifying." Then he encircled the Dharma hall once and went away.

6

One day Ch'an Master Wei-chien of Le-t'an[45] was sitting in meditation at the back of the Dharma hall. The Patriarch saw him sitting, came to him, and blew twice in his ear. Wei-chien emerged from meditation, and when he saw it was the Patriarch, he entered meditation again. The Patriarch went back to the abbot's quarters and asked his attendant to take a bowl of tea to Wei-chien. [When the attendant took the tea to him] Wei-chien ignored him; then he returned to the hall.

7

Ch'an Master Hui-tsang of Shih-kung used to be a hunter [before becoming a monk]. He disliked monks. One day, as he was chasing a herd of deer, he happened to pass in front of the Patriarch's hermitage. The Patriarch greeted him. Hui-tsang asked, "Has the Venerable seen a herd of deer passing nearby?"

The Patriarch asked him, "Who are you?"

Hui-tsang replied, "I am a hunter."

The Patriarch asked, "Do you know how to shoot?"

Hui-tsang said, "Yes, I know."

The Patriarch asked, "How many deer can you shoot with a single arrow?"

Hui-tsang said, "With a single arrow I can shoot only one [deer]."

The Patriarch said, "You don't know how to shoot."

Then Hui-tsang asked, "Does the Venerable know how to shoot?"

The Patriarch said, "Yes, I know."

Hui-tsang asked, "How many can the Venerable shoot with a single arrow?"

The Patriarch said, "With a single arrow I can shoot the whole herd."

Hui-tsang said, "They also have life; why shoot the whole herd?"

The Patriarch said, "If you know that, then why don't you shoot yourself?"

Hui-tsang replied, "If you ask me to shoot myself, I cannot do that."

The Patriarch said, "Ah, this man. All his ignorance and defilements accumulated over vast *kalpas* have today suddenly come to an end." At that point Hui-tsang destroyed his bow and arrows. He cut off his hair with a knife, and became a monk with the Patriarch.

One day, as Hui-tsang was working in the kitchen, the Patriarch asked him, "What are you doing?"

Hui-tsang replied, "I am tending an ox."

The Patriarch asked, "How do you tend an ox?"

Hui-tsang replied, "When he wants to enter the grass, I grab his nostrils and pull him away."

"You are really tending an ox." commented the Patriarch.[46]

## 8

A monk asked the Patriarch, "Without using the four phrases and the hundred negations,[47] may the Venerable directly point out to me the meaning of [Bodhidharma's] coming from the West."

The Patriarch said, "Today I do not feel like doing that. You can go and ask Chih-tsang."[48]

The monk [went to] Chih-tsang and asked the same question. Chih-tsang said, "Why don't you ask the Venerable Master?"

The monk replied, "He sent me here to ask your Reverence."

Chih-tsang rubbed his head with his hand, and said, "I am having a headache today. You can go and ask my elder Dharma-brother Hai."[49]

The monk went to Huai-hai and asked the same question. "I don't know anything about it." was Hui-hai's reply.

Later the monk told the Patriarch what had happened. "Chih-tsang's head is white; Hui-hai's is black." commented the Patriarch.

9

One day as Ch'an Master Pao-ch'e of Ma-ku was accompanying the Patriarch for a walk, he asked, "What is the Great Nirvāṇa?"

"Quickly!" exclaimed the Patriarch.

"What quickly?" asked Pao-ch'e.

"Look at the water." said the Patriarch

10

When Ch'an Master Fa-ch'ang of Ta-mei Mountain went to see the Patriarch for the first time, he asked, "What is Buddha?"

The Patriarch replied, "Mind is Buddha." [On hearing this] Fa-ch'ang had great awakening.

Later he went to live on Ta-mei mountain. When the Patriarch heard that he was residing on the mountain, he sent one of his monks to go there and ask Fa-ch'ang, "What did the Venerable obtain when he saw Ma-tsu, so that he has come to live on this mountain?"

Fa-ch'ang said, "Ma-tsu told me that mind is Buddha; so I came to live here."

The monk said, "Ma-tsu's teaching has changed recently."

Fa-ch'ang asked, "What is the difference?"

The monk said, "Nowadays he also says, 'Neither mind nor Buddha.'"

Fa-ch'ang said, "That old man still hasn't stopped confusing people. You can have 'neither mind nor Buddha,' I only care for 'mind is Buddha.'"

The monk returned to the Patriarch and reported what has happened. "The plum is ripe." said the Patriarch.[50]

## 11

When Ch'an Master Wu-yeh of Fen-chou went to see the Patriarch, the Patriarch noticed that his appearance was extraordinary and that his voice was like [the sound of] a bell. He said, "Such an imposing Buddha hall, but no Buddha in it."

Wu-yeh respectfully kneeled down, and said, "I have studied the texts that contain the teachings of the three vehicles and have been able to roughly understand their meaning. I have also often heard about the teaching of the Ch'an school that mind is Buddha: this is something I have not yet been able to understand."

The Patriarch said, "This very mind that does not understand is it. There is no other thing."

Wu-yeh further asked, "What is the mind-seal that the Patriarch has secretly transmitted from the West?"

The Patriarch said, "The Venerable looks rather disturbed right now. Go and come some other time."[51]

As Wu-yeh was just about to step out, the Patriarch called him, "Venerable!" Wu-yeh turned his head and the Patriarch asked him, "What is it?" [On hearing this] Wu-yeh experienced awakening. He bowed to the Patriarch, who said, "This stupid fellow! What is this bowing all about?"[52]

## 12

When Teng Ying-feng was about to leave the Patriarch, the Patriarch asked him, "Where are you going?"

"To Shih-t'ou." replied Yin-feng.

The Patriarch said, "Shih-t'ou's path is slippery."

Yin-feng said, "I will use my own skills to deal with the situation as it presents itself."[53] Then he left.

As soon as he arrived in front of Shih-t'ou, he walked around the Ch'an seat once, stuck his staff on the ground, and asked, "What is the meaning?"

Shih-t'ou said, "Heavens! Heavens!" Yin-feng was left speechless.

He returned to the Patriarch and reported what has happened. The Patriarch said, "Go back to see him again. When he says, 'Heavens! Heavens!' you make a deep sigh twice."

Yin-feng went back to Shih-t'ou and asked the same question as before. Shih-t'ou made a deep sigh twice. Yin-feng was left speechless again. He returned to the Patriarch and related what has happened.

The Patriarch said, "I told you that Shih-t'ou's path is slippery."

## 13

One day, as Yin-feng was pushing a cart full of dirt, he came across the Patriarch who was sitting [on the ground] with his legs stretched over the path. He said, "Master, please move your legs away."

The Patriarch said, "Since I have already stretched them out, I am not going to move them away."

"Since I am already moving forward, I am not going to retreat." said Yin-feng, and pushed the cart over the Patriarch, thereby injuring his legs.

Later the Patriarch returned to the Dharma hall with an ax in his hand, and asked, "Let the one who injured this old monk's feet step forward." Yin-feng came in front of the Patriarch and stretched out his neck. The Patriarch put the ax down.

## 14

When Venerable Shih-chiu went to see the Patriarch for the first time, the Patriarch asked him, "Where are you coming from?"

Shih-chiu said, "From Wu-chiu."[54]

The Patriarch asked, "What is Wu-chiu talking about these days?"

Shih-chiu said, "How many are uncertain about it?"

The Patriarch said, "Lets leave talking about uncertain, how about saying one sentence quietly."

Shih-chiu stepped three steps forward. The Patriarch said, "I have seven blows with the stick to send to Wu-chiu. Would you be willing to do it for me when you return there?"

Shih-chiu replied, "I will do that if you taste them first." He then returned to Wu-chiu.

## 15

Lecture Master Liang went to see the Patriarch. The Patriarch asked him, "I have heard that the Venerable has been lecturing on many sūtras and *śāstras*. Is that true?"

"Yes." replied Liang.

The Patriarch then asked him, "What do you lecture with?"

Liang replied, "I lecture with my mind."

The Patriarch said, "'The mind is like an actor, consciousness is like a coadjutor.'[55] How can they explain the sūtras?"

Liang said in a raised voice, "If the mind cannot lecture, is it that empty space can lecture?"

The Patriarch said, "Yes, indeed, empty space can lecture."

Liang disagreed with that and [started to] leave. When he was about to step down the stairs, the Patriarch called him, "Venerable lecturer!" Liang turned his head and suddenly had great awakening. He bowed to the Patriarch, who said, "This stupid monk! What are you bowing for?"[56]

Later, when Liang returned to his monastery, he said to the assembly, "I used to think that no one could lecture on the sūtras as well as I did. Today a single question by the Great Master Ma rendered my whole life's work like a melting ice or broken tile."[57] He then returned to the Western Mountain and no trace was found of him afterwards.

## 16

When Venerable Shui-lao of Hung-chou came to see the Patriarch for the first time, he asked, "What is the meaning of [Bodhidharma's] coming from the West?"

The Patriarch said, "Bow down!"

As soon as Shui-lao went down to bow, the Patriarch kicked him. Shui-lao had great awakening. He rose up clapping his hands and laughing heartily, and said, "Wonderful! Wonderful! The source of myriad *samādhis* and limitless subtle meanings can all be realized on the tip of a single hair." He then paid his respects to the Patriarch and withdrew.

Later he told the assembly, "Since the day I was kicked by Master Ma, I have not stopped laughing."[58]

## 17

Layman P'ang asked the Patriarch, "Who is the one that does not keep company with the myriad dharmas?"

The Patriarch said, "I will tell you when you swallow all the water of the West River in a single gulp."[59]

## 18

Layman P'ang also asked, "The unveiled original man asks you to look upward, please." The Patriarch looked straight down. The layman said, "Only the Master can play so wonderfully on a stringless lute." The Patriarch looked straight up. The layman bowed, and the Patriarch returned to his quarters. The layman followed him; when he entered the room, he said, "Just now bungled it trying to be wise."

19

Layman P'ang also asked, "Water has no bones and sinews, and yet it can support a boat of ten-thousand *hu*.[60] What is the meaning of this?"[61]

The Patriarch said, "There is neither water nor boat here; what bones and sinews are you talking about?"

20

A monk asked, "Why does the Venerable say that mind is Buddha?"

The Patriarch said, "To stop small children's crying."

The monk asked, "What do you say when they have stopped crying?"

The Patriarch said, "It is neither mind nor Buddha."

The monk asked, "And when you have someone who does not belong to either of these two, how do you instruct him?"

The Patriarch said, "I tell him that it is not a thing."

The monk asked, "And how about when you suddenly meet someone who is there?"

The Patriarch said, "I teach him to directly realize the Great Way."

21

Someone asked, "What is the meaning of [Bodhidharma's] coming from the West?"

"What is the meaning right now?" replied the Patriarch.

22

A monk asked, "How should one be in harmony with the Way?"

The Patriarch replied, "I am already not in harmony with the Way."

23

Someone asked, "What is the meaning of [Bodhidharma's] coming from the West?"

The Patriarch hit him, and said, "If I don't hit you, people everywhere will laugh at me."

24

There was a young monk whose name was Tan-yüan. Once, after returning from a pilgrimage, he went to the Patriarch and drew a circle in front of him. He then entered the circle, bowed, and stood still. The Patriarch asked him, "Is it that you want to become a Buddha?"

The young monk replied, "I do not know how to rub my eyes."[62]

The Patriarch said, "I am not as good as you." The young monk had no answer.

25

Once a monk drew four lines in front of the Patriarch. The top one was long, the three below were short. He asked, "You may not say that there is one long line and three short lines. Without using the four phrases and the hundred negations, please answer me."

The Patriarch drew one line on the ground and said, "Without talking about long and short, I have answered you."

## 26

The Patriarch sent a monk to deliver a letter to Venerable [Fa-] ch'in of Ching-shan.[63] In the letter he drew a circle. When Ching-shan opened the letter and saw the circle, he took a brush and put a dot in the center.

Later a monk related this to National Teacher Hui-chung.[64] "Master Ching has been fooled by Master Ma." commented the National Teacher.

## 27

Once a lecturing monk came [to the Patriarch], and asked, "What Dharma does the Ch'an school teach?"

[In return] the Patriarch asked him, "What Dharma does the Lecture Master teach?"

The lecturer replied, "I have lectured on over twenty sūtras and *śāstras*."

The Patriarch said, "Aren't you a lion?"

The lecturer said, "Thank you." Thereupon, the Patriarch hissed. The lecturer said, "That is Dharma."

The Patriarch asked, "What Dharma is it?"

The lecturer said, "It is the lion coming out of a cave." The Patriarch kept silent. The lecturer said, "That is also Dharma."

The Patriarch asked, "What Dharma is it?"

The lecturer said, "It is the lion in a cave."

Then the Patriarch asked, "When there is neither coming out nor going in, what Dharma is that?" The lecturer had no reply.[65] He then started to leave. When he reached the door, the Patriarch called him, "Lecture Master!" The lecturer turned his head and the Patriarch asked him, "What is it?" The lecturer had no reply again. "This stupid lecturer." said the Patriarch.

28

The chief law-inspector in Hung-chou asked, "Is it correct to eat meat and drink wine?"

The Patriarch replied, "If you eat meat and drink wine, that is your happiness. If you don't, it is your blessing."

29

When Ch'an Master Wei-yen of Yao-shan[66] went to see Shih-t'ou for the first time, he asked, "I have some knowledge about the three vehicles and the twelve divisions of the teaching. I have also often heard about the Southern [school's] teaching of directly pointing to the mind, perceiving the nature, and becoming a Buddha. This is something I have not been able to understand. May the Venerable be compassionate enough to instruct me."

Shih-t'ou said, "Thus will not do; not thus will not do; either thus or not thus, none will do. What can you say?" Yao-shan was unable to understand. Shih-t'ou said, "Your affinities are not here. Go to the Great Master Ma."

Yao-shan did as he was instructed, and went to see the Patriarch. When he arrived, he bowed respectfully and asked the same question. The Patriarch said, "Sometimes I teach to raise the eyebrows and blink the eyes; sometimes I don't teach to raise the eyebrows and blink the eyes. Sometimes raising the eyebrows and blinking the eyes is correct; sometimes raising the eyebrows and blinking the eyes is not correct. How do you understand this?" On hearing this Yao-shan had an awakening. He bowed to the Patriarch who asked him, "What did you realize so that you are bowing?"

Yao-shan said, "When I was with Shih-t'ou, I was like a mosquito trying to bite an iron ox."

The Patriarch said, "Since you are like this, take good care of it."

Yao-shan stayed with the Patriarch for three years acting as his attendant. One day the Patriarch asked him, "What have your views been recently?"

Yao-shan replied, "All skin has completely come off. There is only one true reality."

The Patriarch said, "What you have attained harmonizes with your mind and is displayed in your four limbs. Since that is so, you can tie three strips of bamboo around your stomach and become the head of a community."

Yao-shan said, "How could I dare to assume that I can become the head of a community?"

The Patriarch said, "That is not so. There has been no one who has always cultivated without starting to teach; there has been no one who has taught without having cultivated himself. If you wish to bring benefits, then there are no benefits. If you wish to act, there is nothing to be done. You should be like a boat. Don't stay here for too long." Soon after this Yao-shan left the Patriarch.

## 30

Ch'an Master T'ien-jan of Tan-hsia[67] went to see the Patriarch. Before going to pay his respects, he entered the monk's hall and rode on the neck of the holy image. The monks started to panic. They quickly went to the Patriarch to report what was happening. The Patriarch went to the hall in person; when he saw Tan-hsia, he said, "My disciple is natural *(t'ien-jan).*"

Tan-hsia came down, paid his respects, and said, "Thank you, Master, for giving me my Dharma-name." This is how he became known as T'ien-jan.

## 31

When Ch'an Master Hui-lang went to see the Patriarch for the first time, the Patriarch asked him, "What are you seeking by coming here?"

Hui-lang replied, "I am seeking for the Buddha's knowledge and insight."[68]

The Patriarch said, "The Buddha has no knowledge and insight; knowledge and insight belong to Māra. Where are you coming from?"

Hui-lang replied, "I am coming from Nan-yüeh."[69]

The Patriarch said, "You are coming from Nan-yüeh, and yet you do not know the essence of the mind of Ts'ao-hsi.[70] You should return there quickly. You need not go to other places."

## 32

The Patriarch asked a monk, "Where are you coming from?"

The monk replied, "I am coming from Hu-nan (South of the Lake)."[71]

The Patriarch asked, "Is the East Lake full?"

The monk replied, "Not yet."

The Patriarch said, "It has been raining for so long; how come it is still not full?"

(Later different monks made comments on the above dialogue.)

Tao-wu said, "Full."[72]

Yün-yen said, "Profound."[73]

Tung-shan said, "In which *kalpa* has it been deficient?"[74]

**NOTES:**

1. In present-day Szechwan province.
2. Long and broad tongue and wheel-signs on the feet are among the thirty-two *lakṣaṇas*, or physical marks, of a Buddha.
3. Tzu-chou is in present-day Szechwan. For Venerable T'ang, also known as Ch'u-chi, see "The Life and Teaching of Ma-tsu" in the Introduction.
4. Nothing is known of this monk. Yu-chou is in present-day Szechwan province.
5. In present-day Hunan province.
6. For Huai-jang, see "The Life and Teaching of Ma-tsu" in the Introduction.
7. The phrase "Dharma-vessel" is used in reference to someone who has the capacity to receive the Dharma and comprehend its meaning.
8. In the *Nirvāṇa Sūtra* the taste of ghee is likened to the perfect teaching, the Buddha-nature, or Nirvāṇa.
9. For the background of this prediction, see the dialogue between Huai-jang and Hui-neng in the Introduction.
10. The other five disciples of Huai-jang are: Ch'ang-hao, Chih-ta, T'an-jan, Shen-chao, and Yen-chun. See CTL *chüan* 5, Huai-jang's entry.
11. In present-day Fukien province.
12. In present-day Kiangsi province.
13. In present-day Fukien province.
14. In present-day Kiangsi province.
15. The literal meaning of the phrase *ju-shih ti-tzu*, which here has been translated as "close disciples," is disciples who have entered (the abbot's) room (to receive personal instructions). This phrase has often been mis-translated to mean enlightened disciples. Putting aside the question of what different translators mean by the word "enlightened," it is difficult to see why all of Ma-tsu's close disciples are necessarily "enlightened." If anything, the masters are repeatedly recorded complaining how difficult it is to find even a single person who understands Ch'an completely. Huang-po puts the number of Ma-tsu's disciples who completely realized his teaching at two or three, and Lin-chi says that for ten or fifteen years he has not been able to find a single man (who understood his meaning).

16. In present-day Kiangsi province.

17. The names of these two Buddhas appear in the *Sūtra of the Buddhas' Names.* The life-span of Sun-face Buddha is said to be one thousand and eight-hundred years, while the life-span of Moon-face Buddha is only one day and one night. This story is case 3 in the *Blue Cliff Record.*

18. Throughout his record, with the exception of the biographical part, Ma-tsu is referred to as the "Patriarch." He is the only Ch'an master, besides the six Chinese patriarchs, who is referred to in such a way, which symbolizes his place of prominence within the Ch'an school. Usually in their records Ch'an masters are referred to as the "Master."

19. This sentence does not appear in any of the three extant Chinese translations of the *Laṅkāvatāra Sūtra.* The phrase "The mind of all the Buddha's teachings" (*i-ch'ieh fo-yü hsin)* is the subtitle of Gunabhadra's translation; Chinese commentators have explained it to mean that among all teachings that the Buddha has expounded, the most essential is the teaching of the mind-ground (*hsin-ti fa-men*). In his work *Treasury of the Proper Dharma-eye,* the Sung Dynasty Ch'an Master Ta-hui Tsung-kao, in his notes on the above passage by Ma-tsu, points out that many students have mistaken this sentence to be a quotation from the *Laṅkāvatāra Sūtra,* and that it has been used as such by both Yung-ming Yen-shou (904-975) in his work *Tsung-ching lu,* and by T'ien-i I-huai (978-1050) in his *T'ung-ming lu.* See HTC vol. 118, p. 18a.

20. Quotation from the "Mañjuśrī Asks for the Illness" chapter, *Vimalakīrti Sūtra.*

21. This quotation appears in the *Fa-chü ching* (T 2901. vol. 85, p. 1432), the title of which suggests it to be one of the Chinese translations of the *Dharmapada,* though probably it is an apocryphal work composed in China. Fa-tsang in his treatise *Contemplation of Practicing the Profound Purport of Avataṃsaka which Extinguishes Falsehood and Returns to the Source,* comments on this passage: "That which is referred to as 'a single Dharma' is the One Mind. This mind includes all mundane and supramundane dharmas. It is the essence of the teaching of the great universal characteristic of the one *dharmadhātu.*" (T 1876. vol. 45, p. 637b).

22. This quotation is from the "Mañjuśrī asks for the Illness" chapter of the *Vimalakīrti Sūtra.* There is a sentence from the

original text which is missing between the second and the third sentence: "These dharmas do not know each other."

23. Quotation from the "Disciples" chapter, *Vimalakīrti Sūtra.*

24. The name of Ocean Seal *Samādhi* (*Sāgara-mudrā Samādhi*) appears in the *Avataṃsaka Sūtra.* According to the Hua-yen tradition this is the *samādhi* in which the Buddha was immersed after his enlightenment, and from which he consequently expounded the *Avataṃsaka Sūtra.* Just as the images of all things are reflected in the still water of the ocean, so are all phenomena manifested within the ocean of Buddha's wisdom. The name of this *samādhi* symbolizes the vastness of the Buddha's awareness. Fa-tsang explains the Ocean Seal *Samādhi* in the following way: "Ocean Seal is the original enlightenment of true suchness. When all falsehood is extinguished the mind becomes clear and still, so that the myriad images equally appear in it. It is like the great ocean whose water has been stirred by wind; when the wind ceases, the water of the ocean becomes clear and still, so that there are no images that are not reflected in it." (T 1876. vol. 45, p. 637b).

25. These two sentences are allusions to a passage from the "Ten Stages" chapter of the *Avataṃsaka Sūtra.* There it is said that the great ocean has ten characteristics; the third characteristic is that when any body of water enters the ocean, it loses its name; the fourth characteristic is that all water in the ocean has a single taste. The third characteristic is a simile for the third stage, the stage of issuing light, in which the Bodhisattva goes beyond conventional names and designations; the fourth characteristic is a simile for the fourth stage, the stage of blazing wisdom, in which the Bodhisattva's merit is of the same taste as the merit of all the Buddhas.

26. The four fruitions of the *śrāvaka* vehicle are stream enterer (*śrota-āpanna*), once returner (*sakṛdāgāmin*), non-returner (*anāgāmin*), and liberated one (*arhat*). The length of their stay in cessation is, according to their attainment, said to be eighty, sixty, forty, and twenty-thousand *kalpas* respectively.

27. Virtuous (or spiritual) friend (*kalyāṇa-mitra*) is someone who by the virtue of his profound insight into the teaching, and the corollary personal transformation, is capable of guiding others along the spiritual path.

28. Quotation from the "Buddha's Way" chapter, *Vimalakīrti Sūtra.*

29. This refers to the ability of the Buddhas and the Bodhisattvas to reproduce their bodies anywhere in the universe.

30. These are the eighteen transmutations that manifest when an *arhat* enters *samādhi.*

31. In Huang-po's treatise *Essentials of the Transmission of Mind* there is the following passage: "Nowadays in this degenerate age there are many who study Ch'an. All of them attach to all kinds of forms and sounds. Why don't they follow our example and let their minds become like empty space; let them become like dry wood, stone, like cold ashes. It is only then that they can have some true attainment."

32. Together with "mind is Buddha," "Ordinary Mind is the Way" became known as the hallmark of Ma-tsu's teaching. See "The Life and Teaching of Ma-tsu" in the Introduction.

33. Quotation from the *Vimalakīrti Sūtra.*

34. The sentence "Unobstructed wisdom is only one" (lit. "is not many") appears in the *Vimalakīrti Sūtra.*

35. The meaning of the Chinese phrase *shan chi hsing,* which here has been translated as "well knowing the nature and characters of all beings," is that the Buddha has the ability to know the particular character of each individual and is able to give a teaching which is best suited to the needs of the person it is given to.

36. Quotation from the "Bodhisattva's Practice" chapter, *Vimalakīrti Sūtra.*

37. This sentence appears in the "Appearance of the *Tathāgata*" chapter of the *Avataṃsaka Sūtra.* The full text of the verse of which it forms a part is:

> If anyone wants to know the mind of all the Buddhas,
> He should contemplate the Buddha's knowledge;
> The Buddha's knowledge has no place of rest,
> Like space which rests on nothing.

38. The analysis of the mind in terms of these two aspects appears in the *Awakening of Faith*, a treatise that has exerted enormous influence on the development of Chinese Buddhism. This whole paragraph is a paraphrase from the treatise. For an English translation of it, see Yoshito S. Hakeda, *The Awakening of Faith* (New York: Columbia University Press, 1967).

39. The literal meaning of the word *Śrāvaka* is "hearer." Originally it was used to refer to those disciples of Buddha who

gained understanding upon hearing his explanations of the doctrine. Bodhisattvas perceive the Buddha-nature with their wisdom-eye. For an interesting discussion on the stage on which Bodhisattvas perceive the Buddha-nature, see Ven. Song-chol, *Echoes of Mt. Kaya* (Seoul: Lotus Lantern International Buddhist Center, 1988), p. 33-35.

40. *Anutpattika-dharma-kṣānti* in Sanskrit. This is an insight of the Bodhisattvas in which they perceive the suchness of all dharmas as being completely disengaged from arising and ceasing. It is attained by the Bodhisattvas on their eight stage, called "immovable" (*acalā*).

41. The sentence "The sūtras enter the treasury" refers to Hsi-t'ang whose Dharma-name is Chih-tsang, *tsang* meaning treasury. "Meditation returns to the sea" refers to Pai-chang whose Dharma-name is Huai-hai, the meaning of the character *hai* being sea. P'u-yüan is the Dharma-name of Nan-ch'üan.

42. Hui-hai is Ta-chu's name.

43. The text simply says "he returned," without specifying the place. Other sources provide the information that Ta-chu returned to his old teacher in Yüeh-chou to attend to his needs as he was getting old and sick.

44. Besides this dialogue nothing else is recorded about this monk.

45. This is the only record of Wei-chien and nothing else is known about him.

46. The use of the image of tending an ox as an allegory for spiritual training is very common in the Ch'an school. On the theme of tending an ox, there is the following exchange between Pai-chang and Ta-an, a disciple of his and the second Abbot of the monastery on Kuei-shan, as recorded in the *Transmission of the Lamp* (CTL *chüan* 9, Ta-an's entry):

> Ta-an asked Pai-chang, "I want to know the Buddha. Who is he?"
>
> Pai-chang said, "It is very much like seeking an ox while you are riding on one."
>
> Ta-an asked, "What shall I do after I know [that]?"
>
> Pai-chang said, "It is like man going home riding on an ox."

Ta-an asked, "How should I take care of it all the time?"

Pai-chang said, "It is like man tending an ox: he looks after it with a stick in his hand and does not let it intrude upon the unripe crops."

Later on, when Ta-an become a teacher in his own right, he told the assembly, "Ta-an has for thirty years been taking the food at Kuei-shan, and then has been returning it at the Kuei-shan's latrine. I did not study Kuei-shan's Ch'an—all I did was looking after a water buffalo. If it went astray from the path and entered the grass, then I would pull it away. If it intruded on other people's crops, I would flog it with a whip in order to tame it. For a long time it was looking miserable, having to listen to a human voice. But now it has become a white ox in an open field, always on my side. Spending the day in the vast open fields, even if someone tries to take advantage of it, it does not go away."

By the time of Sung Dynasty, this allegory started to be used by some Ch'an masters to describe the process of Ch'an training in ten stages, which was to become the famous *Ox-herding Pictures.* This is another instance of "gradual" elements in the Hung-chou school's teaching.

47. The four phrases are existence, emptiness, both existence and emptiness, and neither existence nor emptiness. They are used to elucidate that all phenomena in the universe are unborn. As to the phrase "hundred negations," the number hundred is used to symbolize a very big number, while negations such as not existent, not non-existent, not permanent or impermanent, etc., are used to point out that the ultimate reality is beyond verbal descriptions. In *San-lun hsuan-i*, a treatise by the T'ang Dynasty San-lun school's monk Chia-hsiang, there is the sentence: "If one were to discuss Nirvana, its essence is beyond the four phrases and its reality transcends the hundred negations." The question of the monk can be interpreted to mean: "Without using any form of verbal expression, please point out to me directly the ultimate reality."

48. Hsi-t'ang Chih-tsang.

49. Pai-chang Huai-hai.

50. The character *mei* in the name of the mountain where Fa-ch'ang resided means plum. The meaning of the sentence "The plum is ripe." is that after Fa-chang had his initial awakening, he matured his insight during his cultivation at Ta-mei, and is now ready to start to teach.

51. Later Yün-chu asked, "Where is Fen-chou's (i.e. Wu-yeh's) disturbance?" (CTL *chüan* 8, Wu- yeh's entry).

52. *Sung kao-seng chuan* has a different version of this story, which goes as follows:

> Later, [when Wu-yeh] heard that Ta-chi of Hung-chou was the leader of the Ch'an school, he went there to see him and pay his respects. Wu-yeh's body was six feet tall and it stood magnificently like a mountain. His gaze had a determined expression, and the sound of his voice was like a bell. As soon as he saw him, Ta-chi smiled and said, "Such an imposing Buddha hall, but no Buddha in it."
>
> Wu-yeh respectfully kneeled down, and said, "As to the texts which contain the teachings of the three vehicles, I have been able to roughly understand their meaning. I have also heard about the teaching of the Ch'an school that mind is Buddha; this is something that I have not yet been able to understand."
>
> Ta-chi said, "This very mind that does not understand is it; there is nothing else. When there is no realization, it is ignorance; with realization it is awakening. Ignorance is sentient being; awakening is the Buddha's Way. Without leaving sentient beings, how could there be any Buddha? It is like making a fist with one's hand—the fist is the hand!"
>
> On hearing this Wu-yeh experienced awakening. He wept sorrowfully, and told Ta-chi, "Before I used to think that the Buddha's Way is broad and distant, and that it can be realized only after many *kalpas* of effort and suffering. Today for the first time I realized that the true reality of the

> *dharmakāya* is originally completely present in oneself. All the myriad dharmas are created by the mind and are names only, devoid of any reality."
>
> Ta-chi said, "That is so. The nature of all dharmas is neither born nor perishable. All dharmas are fundamentally empty and quiescent. The sūtras say that 'all dharmas are from the very beginning of the character of extinction [Nirvāṇa].' They also say that they are 'the house of ultimate emptiness and quiescence,' and that 'emptiness is the seat of all dharmas.' That is to say that all the Buddhas, *Tathāgatas*, dwell in this abode of non-dwelling. If one has this understanding, then one dwells in the house of emptiness and quiescence, and sits on the seat of emptiness. Whether lifting the foot or putting it down, one never leaves the site of enlightenment. If upon receiving instructions one has realization, then there is no gradualness; without moving the foot, one ascends to the mountain of Nirvāṇa."

Still another version of the same dialogue can be found in the *Tsu-tang chi*. This version is similar to the one found in the *Record*.

53. The translation is tentative. The literal meaning of the Chinese is something like: "I will have a bamboo pole with me and will perform a play when I get there." I have understood it to be a statement of self-confidence on the part of Yin-feng, claiming that he has his own tricks (a bamboo pole), which he can use to deal with Shih-t'ou (to perform a play) when he gets there.

54. This dialogue is the only extant record of Shih-chiu. In the *Transmission of the Lamp* both he and Wu-chiu are listed as disciples of Ma-tsu. See CTL *chüan* 8.

55. This quotation forms part of a verse which appears in the fourth book of Guṇabhadra's translation of the *Laṅkāvatāra Sūtra*. The full text of the verse is:

> The mind is like an actor,
> Consciousness is like a coadjutor,
> The other five consciousness are like companions,
> False thoughts are like spectators.

The term "mind" in the first line refers to ***alaya-vijñāna,*** the store-consciousness, and the term "consciousness" in the second line stand for ***manas,*** the thinking and calculating mind.

56. In the *Record of Ch'an Master Wen-i*, Fa-yen quotes a slightly different version of this story. According to that account Lecture Master Liang says that he has been lecturing on the *Heart Sūtra*. Then the two texts are in agreement till Liang is about to leave. In Fa-yen's version when Liang responds to Ma-tsu's call, Ma-tsu says, "From birth to old age, it is only this." Fa-yen adds his comment: "It can be seen how compassionate the ancients were when they taught other people. Now, how are you going to understand this? Do not create any false opinions about it!" (T 1991. vol. 47, p. 592c). The *Tsu-tang chi* also contains a variant account of this dialogue which is longer and more elaborate then the other two.

57. The meaning of the phrase "melted ice or broken tile" is that something has been ruined completely.

58. There is a different version of this story in *Ku tsun-su yü-lu* (HTC vol. 118, p. 80d):

> One day, as the Master (Ma-tsu) was gathering rattan [with the community], he saw a puddle of water (*shui-lao*), and made a gesture as if he was going to splash the water. Shui-lao came close to him as if to receive [the water]; the Patriarch kicked him over. Shui-lao rose up laughing heartily, and said, "The source of limitless subtle meanings and myriad *samādhis* can all be realized on the tip of a single hair."

The two versions have different characters for the second character in Shui-lao's name.

59. Before going to see Ma-tsu, layman P'ang went to Shih-t'ou and asked the same question. As soon as he had finished the sentence, Shih-t'ou closed his mouth with his hand. At that the layman had an initial insight. Ma-tsu's reply led him into "sudden awakening to the profound meaning [of Buddhadharma]," an experience that many have interpreted as his final enlightenment.

60. *Hu* is a dry measure 10 or 5 times that of the Chinese peck.

61. *Ku tsun-su yü-lu* has the monk who is participating in dialogue 32 asking this question.

62. This is an allusion to a passage from the second book of

the *Sūraṅgama Sūtra*, where it is said that a second moon which is seen because of the rubbing of the eyes is not to be spoken of as being with or without form, because of its illusory nature. The statement of the young monk can be interpreted to mean: "I am not into creating any illusions."

63. The name of this monk appears in the *Transmission of the Lamp* as Tao-ch'in while the *Biographies of Eminent Monks (Kao-seng chuan)* has it as Fa-ch'in. There are also different dates of his passing away: 719 and 715 respectively. A monk of the Niu-t'ou school of Ch'an, he was a disciple of Hsüan-su. He is regarded as the seventh, and last, patriarch of the Niu-t'ou school.

64. National Teacher Hui-chung (d. 775) was a disciple of the Sixth Patriarch and one of the best known Ch'an masters of his time. Also see the Introduction.

65. Later Pai-chang posed the following reply: "Do you see?" (HTC vol. 118, p. 81b).

66. Ch'an Master Yao-shan Wei-yen (745-828) was a native of Chiang-chou province. His family name was Han. He became a monk at the age of seventeen; Ch'an Master Hui-chao was his first teacher. He received the *bhikṣu* precepts from Vinaya Master Hsin-ts'ao. He studied with both Shih-t'ou and Ma-tsu for a number of years; Ch'an tradition considers him a Dharma successor of Shih-t'ou. Later on he went to live at Yao-shan in Li-chou province and started to teach the numerous students who came to study under him. Among his disciples, the most noted were Tao-wu Yüan-chih (769-835) and Yün-yen T'an-sheng (780-841).

67. Ch'an Master Tan-hsia T'ien-jan (738-823) is considered a Dharma successor of Shih-t'ou. His birth place and family name are unknown. In his young age he studied the Confucian classics. While on his way to the capital of Chang-an to take part in the imperial civil service examinations, he met a Ch'an practitioner who influenced him to give up his pursuit of the career of an official, and instead to go to visit Ma-tsu. Ma-tsu in turn sent him to Shih-t'ou, with whom he eventually became a monk. Later on he visited Ma-tsu again, and also made a number of pilgrimages on which he visited many of the famous Ch'an masters of the time. During one of these travels occurred the famous incident in which on a cold winter day he burned a wooden Buddha-image to warm himself. Finally he settled on Tan-hsia Mountain in Nan-yang (in present-day Kiangsi province), and started to teach.

68. The phrase "the Buddha's knowledge and insight" (*fo chih-chien*) comes from the "Expedient Means" chapter of the *Lotus Sūtra*. There it is said that the Buddha appears in the world for the sake of leading sentient beings to reveal, indicate, realize, and enter the Buddha's knowledge and insight. These three characters can also be interpreted to mean "(intellectual) knowledge and views," which is clearly the way Ma-tsu uses them. While the Buddha's knowledge and insight, the content of which is inconceivable to the unenlightened mind and is not something to be sought with a limited consciousness, is the goal of Ch'an practice, intellectual knowledge and biased views are obstacles to the Path, which is why Ma-tsu places them within the province of Māra.

69. Nan-yüeh has for a long time been a center for Buddhist practice and is the place where Ma-tsu's teacher Huai-jang resided. Here it refers to Shih-t'ou, whose monastery was also on Nan-yüeh. In the *Transmission of the Lamp* Hui-lang is listed as a disciple of Shih-t'ou. According to the same record, after this conversation Hui-lang followed Ma-tsu's advice and returned to Shih-t'ou. See CTL *chüan* 14, Hui-lang's entry.

70. Ts'ao-hsi is the name of the place where the monastery of the Sixth Patriarch is located. So, the phrase "the mind of Ts'ao-hsi" means the mind of the Sixth Patriarch, or simply the enlightened mind.

71. The *Tsu-tang chi* has "Huai-nan," the region south of the Huai River, instead of "Hu-nan" in its version of this dialogue.

72. Yüan-chih of Tao-wu Mountain (769-836), a disciple of Yao-shan. For his biography and teaching, see CTL *chüan* 14.

73. Yün-yen (781-841) is another famous disciple of Yao-shan. He was the teacher of Tung-shan. For more information about him, see CTL *chüan* 14.

74. Tung-shan Liang-chieh (807-869) is the reputed founding teacher of the Ts'ao-tung school of Ch'an. For the text of his record, see HTC vol. 119, p. 437-444, and p. 449-461. For an English translation of it, see William F. Powell, *The Record of Tung-shan* (Honolulu: University of Hawaii Press, 1986).

# *Part Three*
# *Ma-tsu's Disciples*

# *Hsi-t'ang Chih-tsang*

Ch'an Master Hsi-t'ang Chih-tsang (734-814) was a native of Ch'ien-hua.[1] At the age of eight he [left home and] followed his master; at the age of twenty-five he received the full precepts [of a *bhikṣu*]. Later he went to study with Ma-tsu, and together with Pai-chang they were his two close disciples who received his approval. He stayed with Ma-tsu until the latter's death, after which the monks invited him to become abbot and start to teach.

*

One day Ta-chi sent the Master to [the capital of] Chang-an to deliver a letter to National Teacher Hui-chung.[2] The National Teacher asked him, "What is your master teaching?"

The Master walked from east to west, and then stood there.

The National Teacher asked, "Only that? Anything else?"

The Master walked back to the east, and then stood there.

The National Teacher said, "This is what you have learned from Master Ma. How about anything of your own?"

The Master replied, "I have already shown it to the Venerable."

*

One day Ma-tsu asked the Master, "Why don't you study the sūtras?"

The Master replied, "How could the sūtras be different?"

Ma-tsu said, "Though it is so, still, later you will need to use them for the sake of other people."

The Master replied, "Chih-tsang should [first] try to cure his own illnesses; how can he dare to concern himself with other people."

Ma-tsu said, "Later on, you will become well known in the world."

*

Secretary of State Li Ao-ch'ang once asked a monk, "What was the teaching of the Great Master Ma?"

The monk replied, "The Great Master sometimes would say that mind is Buddha; sometimes he would say that it is neither mind nor Buddha."

Li said, "All pass here." Li then asked the Master, "What was the teaching of the Great Master Ma?"

The Master called, "Li Ao!" Li responded. The Master said, "The drum and horn moved."

*

Ch'an Master Chih-kung said to the Master, "The sun is rising too early."

"Just on time." responded the Master.

*

After the Master came to stay at Hsi-t'ang, there was a layman who asked him, "Are there heavens and hells?"

The Master replied, "Yes, there are."

The layman asked, "Are there the [three] treasures of the Buddha, the Dharma; and the Sangha?"

The Master replied. "Yes, there are."

Then the layman asked many questions, on all of which the Master replied in positive.

The layman asked, "Isn't there any mistake in the Venerable speaking this way?"

The Master asked him, "Have you seen any virtuous monks already?"

The layman said, "I went to see Venerable Ching-shan."[3]

The Master asked, "What did Ching-shan have to tell you?"

The layman said, "He said that there are none of those [that I just brought up] at all."

The Master asked him, "Do you have a wife?"

The layman said, "Yes, I do."

The Master asked, "Does Venerable Ching-shan have a wife?"

The Layman replied, "No, he doesn't."

The Master said, "Then it is alright for him to say that there is none."

The layman bowed, thanked the Master, and went away.

**NOTES:**

1. In present-day Kiangsi province.
2. For National Teacher Hui-chung, see "Formation of the Ch'an School" in the Introduction.
3. For Ching-shan see note 63 on the *Record of Ma-tsu.*

# *Pai-chang Huai-hai*

Ch'an Master Huai-hai of Pai-chang Mountain was a native of Chang-le in Fu-chou.[1] His family name was Wang. He left the dust of the world at a young age, and dedicated himself to the three studies.[2] Later on he went to study with Ta-chi, and before long became one of his most prominent disciples. Together with Nan-ch'üan and Hsi-t'ang,[3] they were referred to as "the ones who entered the room."[4] These three great ones stood without peers [among all the disciples of Ma-tsu]. After spending a number of years with Ma-tsu, the Master went to live at Ta-hsiung Mountain in Hung-chou,[5] which because of its steep cliffs was also known as Pai-chang [hundred-foot] Mountain. Before long, students from the four directions came to investigate Ch'an under the Master's guidance; from among his many disciples, the most noted were Kuei-shan and Huang-po. The Master was credited with establishing the first rules for Ch'an monasteries, which later become known as the *Pure Regulations of Pai-chang*.[6] It is said that the Ch'an monastic institutions drew upon the standards set by him for their guidance and inspiration, thereby ensuring his place among the most important Ch'an masters of all times.

*

One day as the Master accompanied Ma-tsu for a walk, they heard a cry of wild duck. Ma-tsu asked, "What kind of sound is that?"

The Master replied, "It is a cry of wild duck."

After a while, Ma-tsu asked, "Where is the sound gone?"

The Master said, "Flown away."

Ma-tsu turned his head, grabbed the Master's nose, and pulled it out. The Master cried with pain. Ma-tsu said, "And yet, you said it has flown away." On hearing that, the Master had an insight.

He returned to the attendant's cottage and started to cry. One of his fellow-monks came in, and asked him, "Are you thinking of your parents?"

"No." replied the Master.

The monk asked, "Has anyone scolded you?"

"No." replied the Master again.

The monk asked, "Then why are you crying?"

The Master said, "The Great Master pulled my nose and it is still hurting."

The monk asked, "What kind of disagreement have you had?"

The Master said, "You can go and ask the Venerable."

The monk then went to Ma-tsu, and asked him, "What has happened so that attendant Hai is crying in the cottage? He told me to ask the Venerable."

Ma-tsu said, "He understands. Go and ask him."

The monk returned to the cottage, and said, "The Venerable said that you understand. He told me to ask you." On hearing that, the Master started to laugh. The monk asked him, "Just a while ago you were crying; why are you laughing now?"

The Master said, "A while ago I was crying; now I am laughing."

The monk could not make anything out of it.

The next day as soon as Ma-tsu entered the Dharma hall and seated himself, the Master stepped forward and rolled up the bowing mat.[7] Ma-tsu then left his seat, and the Master followed him to the abbot's quarters.

Ma-tsu asked, "Concerning what just happened, why did you roll up the bowing mat?"

The Master replied, "Because my nose hurts."

Ma-tsu asked, "Where did you go to?"

The Master said, "Yesterday there was going out and coming in; there is no need to pursue that." Ma-tsu shouted, and the Master left.[8]

*

One day Ma-tsu asked the Master, "Where are you coming from?"

The Master replied, "From the other side of the mountain."

Ma-tsu asked, "Did you meet anyone?"

The Master said, "No, I didn't."

Ma-tsu asked, "Why didn't you meet anyone?"

The Master said, "If I did, I would have told the Venerable."

Ma-tsu asked, "Where did you get this news?"

The Master said, "It is my fault."

Ma-tsu said, "No, it is this old monk's fault."

*

When the Master went to see Ma-tsu again, Ma-tsu took his whisk and held it upright. The Master said, "It is that function; it leaves that function." Ma-tsu put the whisk back at its old place.

After a while, Ma-tsu asked, "Later on, when you open your mouth, what are you going to do for other people?" The Master took the whisk and held it upright. Ma-tsu said, "It is that function; it leaves that function." The Master put the whisk back at its old place. Ma-tsu gave a shout which made the Master deaf for three days.

*

Someone asked the Master, "How can one keep a mind that is like a wood or stone in all kinds of situations?"

The Master said, "All things never say that they are empty, nor do they say that they are form. They also do not say that they are right or wrong, pure or impure. Neither is there any mind to bind anyone. It is only that people themselves create false attachments, thereby giving rise to all kinds of understanding, creating various views, desires, and fears.

"Just realize that all things are not created by themselves—they all come into existence only because of a single false thought that wrongly attaches to appearances. If one perceives that the mind and phenomena do not mutually reach each other, then one is liberated at that very spot. All things are calm and extinct as they are, and that very place is *bodhimaṇḍa*.

"The intrinsic nature cannot be named. Originally it is neither mundane nor holy; it is not pure or impure, empty or existent, good or evil. When among all the defilements, it is called the realm of the two vehicles of humans and gods. If the defiled mind ceases, then there is no abiding in either bondage or liberation. Without any mental conceptions of conditioned and unconditioned, bondage or liberation, though manifesting within the realm of birth and death, one's mind is free. It is ultimately dissociated from all falsehood, illusions, and passions, as well as from the aggregates the realms of sense,[9] birth and death, and the entrances.[10] Having no abode whatsoever, nothing can obstruct it and is free to go or stay. Then the prospect of future births is like an open door."

*

The Master said, "When a person who studies the Way encounters all kinds of painful or pleasant, agreeable or disagreeable situations, his mind does not recede. Not thinking about fame and profit, robes and food, and not being greedy for any merit and blessings, he is not obstructed by anything in the world. With nothing dear, free from love, he can equally accept pain and pleasure. A coarse robe to protect from the cold, simple food to support the body; letting go, like a fool, like a deaf, like a dumb—it is only then that one gains some understanding. If one uses one's mind to broadly engage in intellectual study, seeking merit and wisdom, then all of that is just birth and death, and it does not serve any purpose as far as reality is concerned. Blown by the wind of knowledge, one gets drown in the ocean of birth and death.

"The Buddha is a person who has nothing to seek. If there is seeking, then one is contradicting the principle. The principle is the principle of non-seeking; if one seeks it, one misses it. If one attaches to non-seeking, then that becomes same as seeking; if one attaches to the unconditioned, then it becomes the conditioned again. That is why the sūtra says, 'Not grasping at dharma, not grasping at no-dharma, and not grasping at not no-dharma.' It also says, 'The Dharma attained by the *Tathāgata* is neither real nor false.'[11]

"If one could only for a lifetime keep a mind that is like a wood or stone, without being moved by the aggregates, the realms of sense, the entrances, the five desires,[12] and the eight winds,[13] then one cuts off the cause of birth and death and is free to go or stay. One is not bound by any phenomenal causes and results and is not hindered by any of the afflictions. At that time, because of oneself being free, one can help others by adapting to them and acting in beneficial ways.[14] With an unattached mind one responds to all things; with unobstructed wisdom one unties all bonds. This is what has been called 'Giving medicine according to illness.'"

*

A monk asked the Master, "What is [most] unique?"

The Master said, "Sitting alone on the summit of Ta-hsiung [Mountain]."[15] The monk bowed and the Master hit him.

**NOTES:**

1. Present-day Fukien province.

2. The three studies, or trainings (*triśikṣā*), are *śīla*, or morality; *samādhi*, or mental clarity and composure; and *prajñā*, or non-discriminative insight into the reality of existence, often translated as wisdom.

3. Some versions mention only Pai-chang and Hsi-t'ang, and omit Nan-ch'üan.

4. Meaning that they were his closest and most enlightened disciples.

5. Located in today's Nan-chang in Kiangsi province.

6. For the development and the nature of Ch'an monasticism, as well as for Pai-chang's role in it, see "The Monastic Tradition" in the Introduction.

7. The bowing mat referred to in the text is a kind of bamboo mat which is spread out before the beginning of a Dharma talk by the abbot, and is used by the monks to bow when they ask questions. Since the mat was out, Ma-tsu was going to give a talk; the rolling up of the mat implied that the talk was over. Ma-tsu complied with that, and returned to his quarters.

8. There is another version of the last part of this story in *Ssu-chia yü-lu* (HTC vol. 119, p. 409):

> Ma-tsu asked, "While ago, why did you roll up the mat before I have said anything?"
>
> The Master said, "Yesterday the Venerable grabbed my nose and it is hurting."
>
> Ma-tsu said, "What did you pay attention to yesterday?"
>
> The Master said, "Today my nose does not hurt anymore."
>
> Ma-tsu said, "You have very clearly comprehended yesterday's event."

9. The *dhātus*, of which there are eighteen, are: the six organs, the six sense objects, and the corresponding six consciousnesses.

10. *Ṣaḍāyatana*, the six entrances or locations, can refer to the six sense-organs or to the six objects of cognition which correspond to the six sense-organs.

11. These two quotations are from the *Diamond Sūtra*.

12. The desires for wealth, sex, food and drink, fame, and sleep. The same term can also mean the five objects of sense, viz., form, sound, smell, taste, and physical sensation.

13. The eight winds, or influences, are so called because they stir the mind and cause right awareness to be lost, thereby giving rise to false thinking from which confusion arises. They are gain, loss, scorn, praise, fame, ridicule, suffering, and joy.

14. These two, adaptation to others and beneficial action, together with giving and kind speech, form the four all-embracing virtues, which are different ways of establishing relationship with others that is based on love, respect, and faith. With this kind of trustful relationship, the Bodhisattva is more likely to be able to slowly influence others to listen to his teaching, and then start to practice the Buddha's Path.

15. Ta-hsiung is another name for Pai-chang Mountain. This story forms case 26 of the *Blue Cliff Record.*

# *Nan-ch'üan P'u-yüan*

Ch'an Master P'u-yüan of Nan-ch'üan Monastery (747-834) was a native of Hsin-cheng in Cheng-chou.[1] His family name was Wang. In the second year of Chih-te period (757) he left home and went to study under Ch'an Master Ta-hui of Ta-wei Mountain. During the second year of Ta-li period (777), at the age of thirty, he received the *bhikṣu* precepts from Vinaya Master Kao at Hui-shan Monastery on Sung Mountain.[2] He then studied the ancient writings of the Fa-hsiang school[3] and the Vinaya treatises. Later on he traveled extensively to hear different lectures on the *Laṅkāvatāra Sūtra* and the *Avataṃsaka Sūtra*. He also studied the three main treatises of the San-lun school, the *Madhyamaka Śāstra*, the *Dvādaśanikāya Śāstra*, and the *Śata Śāstra*.[4] After many years of study and practice, he went to Hung-chou to stay with Ma-tsu, and "suddenly forgot the trap and obtained the playful-*samādhi*" (i.e. become free from delusions and worry). From among the over eight-hundred disciples who lived at Ma-tsu's monastery, the Master was considered the most preeminent. During the eleventh year of the Chen-yüan period (795) he went to live at Nan-ch'üan Mountain in Chih-yang county.[5] There he built himself a hermitage, and lived in seclusion supporting himself by working in the mountain. He did not leave the mountain for thirty years. During the beginning of the Tai-ho period (827-835) he was invited to start to teach. Soon many students came to study with him; it is said that his community was never less then several hundreds strong. Among his numerous disciples the most famous were Ch'ang-sha Ching-ts'en (d. 868) and Chao-chou Ts'ung-shen (778-897).

*

Once the Master said, "Ma-tsu taught that mind is Buddha. Elder Master Wang[6] does not say it that way. It is not mind, it is not Buddha, it is not a thing: is there still any fault in this statement?"

Chao-chou bowed and left. One of the monks followed Chao-chou, and asked him, "What did the Venerable mean by bowing and then going out?"

Chao-chou said, "You can go and ask the Abbot."

The monk went back to Nan-ch'üan, and asked, "What did Venerable Shen (Chao-chou) mean [by acting in that way]?"

The Master said, "He understood my meaning."

*

The Master set off together with Kuei-tsung and Ma-ku to go to pay their respects to National Teacher Nan-yang [Hui-chung]. While on the way, the Master stopped, drew a circle on the road, and said, "If you can say something, we will continue." Kuei-tsung sat in the circle; Ma-ku bowed as a woman. The Master said, "Then we don't go."

Kuei-tsung asked, "What kind of thought is that?"

The Master took them back, and they did not go to pay their respects to the National Teacher.[7]

*

When the Master was offering vegetarian meal in memory of the Great Master Ma, he asked the monks, "Is the Great Master Ma going to come?" None of the monks could answer.

Tung-shan said, "He will come when he has a companion."

The Master said, "Though he (i.e. Tung-shan) is still young, he is truly worthy of training."

Tung-shan said, "The Venerable should not disdain a precious thing as being worthless."

*

The Master said, "The old worthy from Kiangsi (i.e. Ma-tsu) used to say that mind is Buddha. Even though the late Patriarch said that mind is Buddha, that was just a statement suited for a particular time. That kind of speech is like an empty fist full of yellow leaves which are used to stop [children's] crying. Nowadays there are many people who say that mind becomes Buddha and wisdom is the Way. They also consider that all seeing, hearing, feeling, and knowing is the Way. Isn't that being like Yajñadatta who sought his head after seeing his reflection in the mirror?[8] Even if he could find something that way, that would still not be his original head. That is why the Bodhisattva scolded Kātyāyana for trying to speak the true Dharma with the mind of birth and death.[9] These are all perverted views. If one says that mind is Buddha, that is like a hare or a horse with horns. If one says that it is neither mind nor Buddha, that is like a cow or a goat without horns. If it is your mind, then what need is there of a Buddha. If he is not without form, then how can he be the Way?"[10]

*

A monk asked, "All the patriarchs till the Great Master from Kiangsi have taught that 'mind is Buddha' and 'Ordinary Mind is the Way.' Now the Venerable says that mind is not Buddha and that wisdom is not the Way. I have certain doubts about it; may the Venerable be compassionate enough to instruct me."

The Master replied in a loud voice, "If you are a Buddha, how can it be that you still have doubts and have to ask this old monk? I am not a Buddha and I have not seen the patriarchs. Since it is you who is speaking in that way, you can go to seek the patriarchs by yourself."

The monk asked, "Since that is so, what kind of teaching can the Venerable offer to help the student?"

The Master said, "Quickly lift the empty space with your palm."

The monk asked, "Empty space has no movable form; how can I lift it?"

The Master said, "When you say that it is without movable form, that is already a movement. How could empty space say 'I have no movable form?' These are all just your perverted views."

The monk asked, "Since [to say that] space is without movable form is just a perverted view, then what did you asked me to lift?"

The Master said, "Since you already know that one cannot speak about lifting it, how are you going to help it?"

The monk asked, "Since 'mind is Buddha' is not correct, is it that mind becomes Buddha?"

The Master said, "'Mind is Buddha' and 'mind becomes Buddha' are just ideas created by your thinking. The Buddha is a person who has wisdom; the mind is the host who collects things. When confronted with things, they perform subtle functions. Do not conceive of mind and do not conceive of Buddha: whatever you conceive of, it becomes an object. This is the so-called 'delusion of knowing.' It is because of this that the Great Master from Kiangsi said, 'It is not mind, it is not Buddha, it is not a thing.' He wanted to teach you, people of later generations, how to act. Nowadays students put on their robes and walk around doubting things that are of no concern to themselves. Have you attained anything that way?"

The monk asked, "Since 'it is not mind, it is not Buddha, it is not a thing' is not correct, what does the Venerable mean when he says 'mind is not Buddha, wisdom is not the Way?'"

The Master said, "Don't consider that mind is not Buddha and that wisdom is not the Way. I have no mind to bring up; what are you going to attach to?"

The monk asked, "If there is nothing at all, then in which way is it different from empty space?"

The Master said, "Since it is not a thing, how can you compare it to empty space? Also, who spoke of sameness and difference?"

The monk said, "It cannot be that now 'it is not mind, it is not Buddha, it is not a thing' is not right!"

The Master said, "If you understand it that way, it just becomes 'mind is Buddha' again."

**NOTES:**

1. In present-day Honan province.

2. Sung-shan is the highest and central peak of the Five Sacred Mountains of China, located in Honan province. The famous Shao-lin Monastery, where Bodhidharma is said to have sat for nine years in front of a wall, is on this mountain.

3. Fa-hsiang, or Dharma-lakṣaṇa, is the Chinese version of the Yogācāra school, sometimes also called "Wei-shih tsung," Consciousness-only school. Its teachings are based on the *Vijñānavāda* (Mind-only) doctrines of the great Indian monks Vasubandhu, Asaṅga, and Dharmapāla. Its teachings were transmitted to China by Hsüan-tsang during the early T'ang Dynasty; his disciple K'uei-chi of Tz'u-en Monastery is regarded as the founder of this school.

4. These three treatises were translated in Chinese by Kumārajīva. They are the main texts of the Chinese equivalent of the Mādyamika school, the "Three Treatises" school (San-lun tsung). The first two were written by Nāgārjuna, while the third is attributed to Āryadeva.

5. In present-day Honan province.

6. Wang is Nan-ch'üan's lay surname. He often uses it to refer to himself as "Elder Master Wang."

7. This story forms case 69 of the *Blue Cliff Record*. For the interview between Nan-ch'üan and Hui-chung, see CTL *chüan* 5, Hui-chung's entry.

8. The story of Yajñadatta is told in the fourth book of the *Sūraṅgama Sūtra*. There it says that one day he looked into a mirror and saw his eyebrows and eyes, but not seeing them on his head, he went mad and started walking around looking for his head.

9. Kātyāyana was one of the ten great disciples of the Buddha, foremost in expounding the doctrine. In the "Disciples" chapter of the *Vimalakīrti Sūtra* he is reproved by Vimalakīrti for speaking the true Dharma with the mind of birth and death.

10. It seems that Nan-ch'üan here is trying to counteract some of the misunderstandings upheld by part of Ma-tsu's followers concerning Ma-tsu's statement "mind is Buddha." As pointed out by Tsung-mi, the unqualified emphasis on the dynamic aspect of the true mind may lead to partial view, which neglects its transcendent aspect. Here Nan-ch'üan tries to balance that view by pointing to the relative (empty) nature of both the dynamic (manifest) and the transcendent aspects of the True Mind. See "Tsung-mi's Evaluation of the Hung-chou School" in the Introduction.

# *Ta-chu Hui-hai*

Ch'an Master Ta-chu was a native of Chien-chou.[1] His family name was Chu. He left home and started studying Buddhism under Venerable Tao-chih of Ta-yün Monastery in Yüeh-chou.[2] Later on he went to Kiangsi and became a disciple of Ma-tsu. He stayed with Ma-tsu for six years, after which he returned to Yüeh-chou to take care of his aging teacher. During that time he composed a treatise entitled: *Discourse on the Essentials of Entering the Way Through Sudden Awakening (Tun-wu ju-tao yao-men lun)*.[3] It was only after Ma-tsu saw the text and approved of it that Ta-chu started to teach.

*

A cultivator asked the Master, "[It is said that] mind is Buddha, but which one is [the true] Buddha?"

The Master said, "Can you point something that you think is not Buddha?" The cultivator had no reply. The Master added, "If you have realization, then everything is Buddha; if you haven't had awakening, then you will be far away from it forever."

*

The Master said, "The Venerable from Kiangsi (i.e. Ma-tsu) once told me: 'Your own treasure is completely endowed with all that you need, and you are free to use it. You don't have to seek outside.'[4] Since that time I have been at rest. Being able to use one's treasure according to one's needs can truly be called a happy life. There is not a single thing to grasp, nor is there a single thing to reject. When you do not perceive anything as having birth or death, and do not see anything as either coming or going, then within the whole universe there is not a speck of dust that is not your own treasure.

"Just observe your mind carefully—from a single essence, the three treasures are always manifested within;[5] there is nothing to be anxious about. Because the mind's nature is fundamentally pure, there is nothing to ponder over, nothing to seek.

"It is said in the *Avataṃsaka Sūtra*: 'All dharmas are not born, all dharmas do not cease. If you can understand this, then all the Buddhas will manifest themselves.' Moreover, it is said in the *Vimalakīrti Sūtra:* 'As contemplating the reality of the body, the Buddha should also be contemplated thus.' If you do not give rise to any thinking due to sounds and forms, and do not by pursuing appearances create any understanding, then naturally there is nothing to do. You have been standing long enough. Take care!"

*

Someone asked, "Is *prajñā* big?"
The Master said, "It is big."
The questioner asked, "How big is it?"
The Master said, "It is without limits."
The questioner further asked, "Is *prajñā* small?"
The Master said, "Yes, it is."
The questioner asked, "How small is it?"
The Master said, "So small that it cannot be seen."
The questioner asked, "Where is it?"
The Master said, "Where is it not?"

*

There was a cultivator who once asked the Master, "How can one abide in the right Dharma?"

The Master said, "To seek to abide in the right Dharma is wrong. Why? Because the Dharma is beyond right and wrong."

The cultivator asked, "How can one become a Buddha?"

The Master said, "There is no need to abandon the mind of sentient being—just do not defile your self-nature. The sūtra says, 'Mind, Buddha, and sentient beings are not different from each other.'"[6]

The cultivator asked, "If one has this kind of understanding, is he going to obtain liberation?"

The Master replied, "Since originally you are not bound, there is no need to seek liberation. The Dharma is beyond words and letters: do not seek it in verbal expressions. The Dharma is not of past, present and future: you cannot unite with it within the realm of cause and effect. The Dharma is transcendental and beyond comparison. The *dharmakāya* is without form, and yet it can manifest forms in response to things. Liberation is not to be sought outside of this world."

**NOTES:**

1. Present-day Ch'ien-ou district in Fukien province.
2. Present-day Shao-hsing district in Chekiang province.
3. For an English translation of this treatise and the record of Ta-chu's life and teaching, see John Blofeld, *The Zen Teaching of Hui Hai on Sudden Illumination* (London: Rider & Company, 1962).
4. See the dialogue between Ma-tsu and Ta-chu in the "Record of Ma-tsu" in this volume (dialogue 4).
5. The three treasures are the Buddha, the Dharma, and the Sangha. These three are different aspects of one reality, hence the expression *i-t'i san-pao*, "three treasures of a single essence."

6. This quotation is from the "Verses Spoken by the Bodhisattvas in the Palace of Suyāma Heaven" chapter of the Buddhabhadra's translation of the *Avataṃsaka Sūtra*. The text of the verse of which it forms a part is:

As Mind is, so is Buddha;
As Buddha is, so are sentient beings.
Mind, Buddha, and sentient beings
Are not different from each other.

# *Shih-kung Hui-tsang*

(For the story of Shih-kung's awakening, see the *Record of Ma-tsu,* dialogue 7.)

The Master asked Hsi-t'ang, "Do you know how to grasp empty space?"

Hsi-t'ang said, "Yes, I know."

The Master asked, "How can you grasp it?"

Hsi-t'ang made a gesture as if trying to grasp the space with his hand. The Master said, "How can you grasp empty space in that way?"

Hsi-t'ang asked, "How is my elder Dharma-brother going to grasp it?"

The Master grabbed Hsi-t'ang's nostril and pulled it. Hsi-t'ang cried with pain, and said, "You are pulling my nostril to death. Stop it immediately!"

The Master said, "This is the way to grasp empty space."

*

Once a group of monks came to see the Master. The Master asked, "Where did it go right now?"

One of the monks said, "It is here."

The Master asked, "Where is it?"

The monk snapped his fingers once.

*

A monk came to bow. The Master asked him, "Did you bring that back?"

The monk said, "Yes, I brought it back."

The Master asked, "Where is it?"

The monk snapped his fingers thrice.

*

A monk asked, "How can one escape from birth and death?"

The Master said, "Why do you want to escape from them?"

The monk asked [again], "How can one escape from them?"

The Master said, "This one has no birth and death."

# *Ma-ku Pao-ch'e*

Once, while the Master was walking in the mountains together with Tan-hsia,[1] he saw a fish in the water. He pointed it to Tan-hsia.

Tan-hsia said, "Natural. Natural."

The next day the Master asked Tan-hsia, "What did you mean yesterday?" Tan-hsia lay down on the ground. The Master said, "Heavens!"

*

On another occasion the Master and Tan-hsia arrived at Ma-ku Mountain. The Master said, "I am going to stay here."

Tan-hsia said, "Let you stay if you wish, but is there still any of that?"

The Master said, "Take good care."

*

A monk asked, "I don't doubt the twelve divisions of the teaching; what is the meaning of the Patriarch's coming from the West?"

The Master stood-up, went with the stick around his body once, lifted his foot, and said, "Do you understand?" The monk had no reply. The Master hit him.

*

A monk asked, "What is the great meaning of Buddhadharma?" The Master kept silent.

The same monk later asked Shih-shuang,[2] "What was the meaning of that?"

Shih-shuang said, "The host is busy getting others involved in combat. It is only that you are too confused."[3]

*

Tan-yüan asked the Master, "Is the twelve-headed Kuan-yin an ordinary person or a sage?"

The Master said, "A sage." Tan-yüan hit the Master.

The Master said, "I knew that you have not reached that realm."

**NOTES:**

1. For Tan-hsia see dialogue 30 in the *Record of Ma-tsu.*

2. Shih-shuang Ta-shan was another disciple of Ma-tsu. Once when he was asked the same question, he replied, "On a spring day a cock crows." When the monk remonstrated that he does not understand, Shih-shuang said, "In Mid-Autumn a dog barks." See CTL *chüan* 8, Shih-shuang's entry.

3. The literal reading of the Chinese is "to drag through mud and water," meaning confused, sloppy, unable to make decisions; hence the translation "too confused."

# *Ta-mei Fa-ch'ang*

Ch'an Master Fa-ch'ang of Ta-mei Mountain in Ming-chou was born in Hsiang-yang.[1] His family name was Cheng. While still very young, he become a monk at Yü-chuan Monastery in Ching-chou province.

The first time he went to see Ta-chi, he asked, "What is Buddha?"

Ta-chi said, "Mind is Buddha." The Master had great awakening.

During the Chen-yüan period of the T'ang Dynasty (785-805) he went to live on Ta-mei Mountain, seventy miles south of Yin county, at the place where in ancient times Mei Tzu-chen had his retreat.

Once, as a monk from the Yen-kuan's[2] community entered the mountain to gather wood, he got lost, [and while he was trying to find his way] he came across the Master's hermitage. He asked, "How long has the Venerable been living on this mountain?"

The Master replied, "I can only see the four mountains turning green and yellow."

Then the monk asked, "Which is the way out of the mountain?"

The Master said, "Just follow the stream."

The monk returned to Yen-kuan and reported what had happened. Yen-kuan said, "When I was in Kiangsi, I met a monk of whom I have not heard ever since. Is it possible that he is that monk?" He then sent a monk to invite the Master to leave the mountain.

The Master composed a verse:

A broken dry wood lying in a cold forest,
How many springs has it met without a change of
heart?
Even when the wood-cutter passes by, he does not
look at it;
How could a man from Ying seek for it?[3]

*

The Master gave the following talk to the assembly: "All of you should turn your mind to penetrate the source; do not follow the apparent. If you realize the source, the apparent will be accomplished naturally. If you wish to know the source, you only need to realize your own mind. Originally this mind is the source of all mundane and supramundane dharmas. That is why, 'when the mind arises, various kinds of dharmas arise; when the mind ceases, the various dharmas cease.' When the mind functions without attaching to either good or evil, then the myriad dharmas are themselves suchness."

*

Layman P'ang asked the Master, "For a long time I have been looking towards Ta-mei.[4] Is the plum ripe already?"

The Master said, "Where would you like to bite?"

Layman P'ang said, "If that is so, then it is so many complicated trifles."

The Master said, "Return me the kernel."

*

A monk asked, "What is the great meaning of Buddhadharma?"

The Master said, "Rush flowers, willow catkins, bamboo needle, and hemp thread."

*

Once Chia-shan and Ting-shan had a conversation while walking together. Ting-shan said, "If in birth and death there is no Buddha, then that is not birth and death."

Chia-shan said, "If while in birth and death there is Buddha, then one is not deluded by birth and death."

When the two of them came to visit the Master, after paying their respects, Chia-shan related their conversation, and asked the Master, "Among the two of us, which one is closer [to the truth]?"

The Master said, "One is close, one is distant."

Chia-shan asked, "Which one is close?"

The Master said, "Go now. Come back tomorrow."

The next day Chia-shan came again and asked the same question. The Master said, "The one who is close does not ask; the one who asks is not close."[5]

(Later Chia-shan commented: "At that time I lost a single eye.")

*

One day the Master unexpectedly said to his disciples, "Coming, it cannot be resisted; going, it cannot be pursued."

At that time they heard a sound of a flying squirrel. The Master said, "It is just this; not something else. All of you should take good care of it. Now I am departing." Having said that, he passed away. He was eighty-eight years old, and had been a monk for sixty-nine years.

**NOTES:**

1. Present-day Hsiang-yang county in Hupeh province.

2. Yen-kuan was another disciple of Ma-tsu. For an account of his teaching, see CTL *chüan* 7.

3. Ying was the name of the capital of the state of Chu during the period of Spring and Autumn (722-481/480) in today's Hupeh province.

4. The meaning of Ta-mei is "great plum," and it can refer both to the monk and to the mountain. This conversation happened sometime after the one described in dialogue 11 in the *Record of Ma-tsu*. Probably Layman P'ang had heard that Ma-tsu acknowledged Ta-mei's understanding by saying "the plum is ripe," and he wanted to check Ta-mei by himself.

5. This is an allusion to the opening passage of section 56 of *Tao-te ching*, which reads: "The one who knows does not speak; the one who speaks does not know."

# *Fen-chou Wu-yeh*

Ch'an Master Wu-yeh of Fen-chou (761-823) was a native of Shang-lo in Shang-chou province. His family name was Tu. He was an unusual child: when walking he always looked straight ahead, and when seated he would always cross his legs in the posture for meditation. At the age of nine he started to study the Mahāyāna sūtras under the guidance of Ch'an Master Chih-pen; among the texts he studied were the *Diamond Sūtra,* the *Lotus Sūtra,* the *Vimalakīrti Sūtra,* and the *Avataṃsaka Sūtra*. At the age of twelve he had his head shaved, and when he became twenty he received the *bhikṣu* precepts from the Vinaya Master Yu of Hsiang-chou. He then studied the commentaries of the *Four-division Vinaya,*[1] and was able to lecture on them as soon as he had finished reading them. He would always lecture on the *Mahāparinirvāṇa Sūtra,* regardless of it being summer or winter. Later on, he heard that Ma-tsu was the leader of the Ch'an school in Hung-chou, and went to study with him.[2] After receiving Ma-tsu's seal of approval, he went to Ts'ao-hsi to pay his respects to the stūpa of the Sixth Patriarch. From there he continued his pilgrimage to Lu-shan, Nan-yüeh, T'ien-t'ai, and other holy mountains. While he was resting at Hsi-ming Monastery on his way to Yung, the monks there invited him to become the leader of the community. The Master declined the invitations saying that was not his original intention. Later on he went to Shang-tang where the provincial governor Li Pao-chen held him in high esteem and paid him frequent visits. The Master always had a weary expression; he said, "Originally I kept myself away from the great crowds around the court. How could I now like to trouble myself with contacts with the potentate." Consequently the Master left. After a short stay at Pao-fu Mountain in Mien-shang, he went to Chin-ko Monastery in Ch'ing-liang. There he spent eight years in reading the whole *tripiṭaka*. After that he moved south to the West River, where he was invited by Tung Shu-ch'an, the district magistrate, to stay at K'ai-yüan Temple. The Master said to his disciples, "Since my arrival here, I haven't had any intent to travel to other places. It seems my affinities lie here." From then on he started to teach and for twenty years he instructed all the people in Fen-chou.[3] Whenever students came to him, he would simply say, "Don't indulge in false thinking."

Emperor Hsien-tsung of T'ang (r. 805-821) heard about the Master and sent an invitation for him to appear at the court. The Master did not comply with the request, offering illness as an excuse. The same happened the next year. When the next emperor Mu-tsung (r. 821-825) succeeded to the throne, he sent messengers to invite the Master to come to the capital, so that the Emperor can pay him his respects. When the messengers arrived at Master's monastery, they informed him about the Emperor's anxiety to see him and requested that this time he does not feign illness. The Master smiled, and said, "What virtue does this poor monk have so that he can dare to cause worry to the Emperor. You can return now; I will come another way." He then shaved his head, took a bath, and when the middle of the night arrived, he said to his disciples, "This very nature of yours that does see, hear, feel, and know, is the same age as empty space which is neither born nor perishable. All objects are fundamentally empty and quiescent; there is not a single thing that can be obtained. The ignorant lack realization, and are thereby deluded by objects, transmigrating in *saṃsāra* without an end. You should know that the nature of your mind is intrinsically present; it is not something produced. It is like a diamond which is indestructible. All things are like shadows and echoes, devoid of any reality. That is why the sūtra says, 'It is only this one that is true; the others are not real.' You should always live in the realization that everything is empty, that there is nothing one needs to ponder about: this is the way all the Buddhas use their minds. You should diligently cultivate this." Having said this, he passed away while sitting cross-legged. He was sixty-two years old, and had been a monk for forty-two years. He received the posthumous title National Teacher Ta-ta (Great Penetration). The stūpa built in his memory was called Ch'eng-yüan.

*

There was a monk who asked the Master, "The twelve divisions of the teaching have spread through this land; the number of those who have obtained the fruits of the Way does not stop at one or two. How is it that the Patriarch has come to the East and has proclaimed a separate mysterious teaching which directly points to the human mind, whereby one can perceive one's nature and become a Buddha. How is it possible that there is something missing in the teachings that the *Bhagavat* has spoken? In the past all virtuous high monks thoroughly studied the nine orifices and clearly penetrated the teachings of the *tripiṭaka*. Tao-sheng, Seng-chao, Tao-jung, Seng-jui: all of them were extraordinary people.[4] How can it be that they did not understand Buddhadharma? May the Master be kind enough to instruct this ignorant person."

The Master said, "All the Buddhas have not appeared in the world, nor has there been a single teaching that they have given to people. The twelve divisions of the teaching are like medicines that are used to cure various diseases. It is like sweet fruit used to change [the taste of] bitter calabash. They are all for the sake of cleaning away your karma—there is nothing real about them. The spiritual powers and transformations, as well as hundreds and thousands of *samādhis* are for the sake of converting the heavenly demons and the heretics. The two adornments of blessings and wisdom are for the sake of destroying the views of attachment to existence and abiding in emptiness. If one does not understand the Way and the meaning of the Patriarch's coming [from the West], then what use is there in speaking about Tao-sheng, Seng-chao, Tao-jung, and Seng-jui. Nowadays those who explain Ch'an and explain the Way are as many as the sands of Ganges. Those who speak about Buddha and mind count in millions. If there is even a tiny speck of dust remaining, then one still has not left the wheel [of birth and death]. If all thinking is not gone, then one is certain to fail completely. These kind of people don't themselves understand about cause and effect, and falsely speak about benefiting oneself and benefiting others. They consider themselves to be superior people equal to the former worthies. They say that whatever comes in contact with the eye is Buddha activity, and that wherever the foot is set is *bodhimaṇḍa*. Their original practice cannot be compared even with that of an ordinary person who only keeps the five precepts[5] and the ten wholesome ways of action.[6] When they start speaking, they slight those of the two vehicles and the Bodhisattvas of the ten stages. Though the superior taste of ghee is considered rare and precious in the world, when it comes in contact with these it turns into poison. Even Nan-shan[7] didn't allow to call himself Mahāyāna.

"All those who are engrossed in studying words, when arguing with eloquence they loudly discuss that which is without form. It is so pitiable when compared with the ancient worthies. Like a gentleman of noble character who gives up his wealth and position, and goes to live in the wilderness, using a stone as a pillow and a stream to rinse himself. Though he has the ability to pacify the country and govern the people, when called [by the emperor] he refuses to go.

"The way of our Ch'an school is different. After the ancient worthy people of the Way attained realization, they went to live in thatched huts and stone houses. They would use old cauldron with broken legs to cook their food, and would pass twenty or thirty years in that way. Unconcerned about fame and wealth, they never thought of money and riches. Completely forgetting about human affairs, they concealed their traces among the rocks and thickets. When summoned by the monarch, they would not respond; when invited by the princes, they would not go. How can they be same as those who, greedy for fame and desirous for wealth, sink into the worldly ways. It is like a peddler who by seeking small profit loses great gain. If the sages of the ten stages have not realized the principle of the Buddhas, then wouldn't they be like ordinary people with great learning? There is no such thing really.

"Even though he could speak the Dharma as eloquently as clouds and rain, he was still scolded by the Buddha, who said, 'Seeing the nature is like dividing thin silk.' As long as there is feeling of holiness, and views about cause and effect, one has still not been able to transcend the feeling of sacredness nor go beyond shadows and traces. The former sages and ancient worthies were eminent people of great learning who were familiar with the past and the present, and had clear insight into the Teaching. Yet, despite all of their learning and eloquence, they still could not distinguish between milk and water. Not knowing themselves, they sought reality by calming their thoughts.

"Alas! Those who obtain human body are like dirt on nail; those who lose it are like the great earth. This is really something to grieve about.

"There might be someone who has awakened to the principle, and yet still has certain knowledge and understanding. Because of not knowing that within awakening one enters the principle, he considers himself as being beyond worldly advantage.[8] Walking through mountains and sitting besides streams, he slights the path to Nirvāṇa.

"If one's mind is not completely free from outflows, and one is not clear about the fundamental reality, then one's whole life will be wasted without accomplishing anything. Karma cannot be overcome by cleverness; dry wisdom cannot help one to escape the wheel of suffering. Even if one has eloquence equal to that of Aśvaghoṣa, or understanding like that of Nāgārjuna,[9] one can still avoid losing the human body for only lifetime or two. Profound thoughts, innate purity, ability for immediate comprehension—just like Tao-sheng—all of that is not something to be envious about, because that is still far away from the Way.

"Brothers! What I say is true, not false. Your eating of food and wearing robes is just cheating the sages and deceiving the saints. If you are considering the future, those with the eye of wisdom will perceive this like eating pus and blood. One day you will still have to repay others. Those who attain the fruit of the Way are naturally able to refuse the donors when they come with offerings.

"Bodhisattvas who study *prajñā* do not deceive themselves. They are like someone who is walking on ice or on the blade of a sharp sword. If at the time of one's death one still has any feeling of ordinary or holy that has not been let go of, any subtle thought that has not been forgotten, then one receives birth according to one's thoughts. Corresponding to the heaviness or lightness of one's karma, one is reborn in the womb of a donkey or a horse, or in the hell of cauldrons of molten iron. At that time all one's former practices, thoughts, views, and wisdom will be lost in an instant. And then one is again reborn as a mole cricket or an ant, only to be reborn as a mosquito or a gadfly again. Though there is a good cause, the result is nevertheless bad. Why do that?

"Brothers! If you cherish any desires, then you will be tied down to the twenty-five abodes of living beings,[10] never accomplishing anything.

"The Patriarch [Bodhidharma] perceived that the people of this country had the potential for receiving Mahāyāna, so he only pointed to people's confused feelings and transmitted the mind-seal. If one attains this, then one does discriminate between ordinary and holy, ignorance and wisdom. A lot of falsehood is not as good as a bit of truth.

"The true person should right now strait go to rest. Suddenly putting to rest the myriad conditions, one transcends the stream of birth and death, and, going beyond rules and patterns, the spiritual light shines solitary. Not hindered by things and events, dignified and upright, one walks alone in the three realms. What need then there is of a sixteen feet body with a golden skin radiating bright color, halo around the head, broad and long tongue?[11] 'If one sees me through forms, he seeks the false way.'[12] Then even without seeking them, retinues and various adornments are naturally present, and mountains, rivers, and the great earth cannot hinder one's sight. One attains the great *dhāraṇī,* and is able to understand thousand [meanings] on a single hearing. One is not seeking even as much as the value of a single meal.

"If you are not like this, then the Patriarch's coming to this land has brought both benefit and loss. As to benefit, among hundreds and thousands of people, one can pick one, or half, who is a Dharma-vessel. As to loss, that has been explained already. Let then them practice according to the teachings of the three vehicles, so that they can obtain the four fruits and the three virtuous stages,[13] thereby making some progress in their practice. That is why a former worthy has said, 'If one has realization, then [one perceives that] the karmic obstacles are fundamentally empty; without realization, one still has to repay one's debts.'"

**NOTES:**

1. This is the Chinese translation of the Vinaya of the Dharmagupta school, done in 405 by Buddhayaśas and Chu Fonien. It is so called because it is comprised of four sections. This is the Vinaya that has been, and still is, used by all Chinese monks and there are numerous works on it.

2. For the story of Wu-yeh's meeting with Ma-tsu, see the *Record of Ma-tsu,* dialogue 11.

3. In present-day Shansi province.

4. Tao-sheng (360-434), Seng-chao (384-414), Tao-jung (n.d.), and Seng-jui (355-498) are the four great disciples of Kumārajīva. The better known two are Seng-chao, who is the author of *Chao lun,* a collection of essays which was later widely read in Ch'an circles and exerted considerable influence on the thought of many Ch'an masters; and Tao-sheng, who was the first to propound the theories of universal Buddhá-nature and sudden enlightenment.

5. The five precepts are to abstain from killing, stealing, improper sexual relationships, lying, and consuming alcoholic beverages.

6. The first four of the ten wholesome ways of action are identical with the fist four of the five precepts. The remaining are to eschew slander, use of offensive language, equivocation, avarice, anger, and ignorance.

7. Tao-hsüan (596-667), the founder of the Vinaya school in China who lived on Nan-shan, and is known as Nan-shan Ta-shih. He wrote five important treatises on the Vinaya, and he is also the author of *Hsü kao-seng chuan (Additional Biographies of Eminent Monks).*

8. This passage describes a common mistake in the practice when one experiences certain shallow insight into the nature of reality ("awakened to the principle") which is still tainted by various forms of intellectual understanding. Because of the obstructions created by this knowledge, one is unable to enter into the reality, while considering oneself to be an enlightened person. It is like someone who has only seen the door, without actually going through it and entering the realm beyond.

9. Aśvaghoṣa and Nāgārjuna are among the most famous and respected monks in the Indian tradition. Aśvaghoṣa was best known in China as the author of *Buddhacarita kāvya sūtra,* a poetic narrative of the Buddha's life, and the *Awakening of Faith.* Nāgārjuna is the reputed founder of the Mādhyamika school. He is the greatest philosophical genius of the Mahāyāna tradition, and all schools of Chinese Buddhism trace their lineages back to him.

10. The twenty-five abodes of living beings are: the four evil realms, the four continents of the human realm, the six heavens

of the realm of desire, the seven heavens of the realm of form, and the four heavens of the formless realm.

11. These are some of the physical marks of a Buddha.

12. Quotation from the *Diamond Sūtra*.

13. The three virtuous stages of a Bodhisattva are the ten abidings, the ten practices, and the ten dedications. Their most comprehensive and authoritative explication can be found in the *Avataṃsaka Sūtra*.

# *Wu-tai Yin-feng*

Ch'an Master Yin-feng was from Shao-wu in Fukien province. His family name was Teng. As a child he didn't show great intelligence, and his parents allowed him to become a monk. First he studied with Ma-tsu, but was unable to perceive the profound mystery. Later on he went to Shih-t'ou. Though in his study with both masters he did not make a very rapid progress, later on he gained realization on hearing Ma-tsu's words.

*

When the Master was with Shih-t'ou, he asked, "How should one unite with the Way?"

Shih-t'ou said, "I am also not in union with the Way."

The Master asked, "Ultimately, how is it?"

Shih-t'ou said, "How long have you been with this?"

*

When the Master arrived at Nan-ch'üan he saw the monks assembled together. Nan-ch'üan pointed to a pitcher, and said, "This bronze pitcher is an object. In the pitcher there is water. Without moving the object, bring the water to this old monk."

The Master took the pitcher and poured the water in front of Nan-ch'üan. Nan-ch'üan did not say anything.

*

Later on, when the Master arrived at Kuei-shan,[1] he put his robe and bowl on the head monk's seat. When Kuei-shan heard that his younger Dharma-brother had come, he formally went to the hall to meet him. When the Master saw him, he lay down as if asleep. Kuei-shan returned to his quarters, and the Master started to leave. A bit later, Kuei-shan asked his attendant, "Is my younger Dharma-brother still here?"

The attendant told him, "He is already gone."

Kuei-shan asked, "What did he say when he left?"

The attendant replied, "He didn't say anything."

Kuei-shan said, "Don't say he didn't say anything. His voice was like a thunder."

*

Later on the Master went to live on Wu-t'ai Mountain.[2] When he was about to pass away in front of the Diamond Cave, he asked the monks, "I have already seen people passing away while sitting or lying. Has there been anyone who has passed away standing?"

The monks answered, "Yes, there has been."

The Master asked, "And how about anyone passing away while standing on his head?"

The monks said, "We have not heard of anyone."

The Master then stood on his head and passed away. He looked dignified and his robe stayed properly attired on his body. When the monks decided to lift the body and take it away for cremation, the body was still standing erect and it was impossible to move. People from near and far came to see this. Everyone greatly marveled at this occurrence.

The Master had a sister who was a nun. When she came to the body, she bowed, came close, and shouted, "Brother! While alive you didn't comply with the Dharma-Vinaya; even after your death you are still confusing people." She then pushed the body with her hand and the body fell flat on the ground. Soon afterwards the body was cremated. The *śarīras* were placed into a pagoda.

**NOTES:**

1. The mountain where Kuei-shan Ling-yu, a disciple of Pai-chang and one of the most famous Ch'an monks, resided. The Kuei-yang school of Ch'an took him as its founding master.

2. Wu-t'ai shan is one of the four holy Buddhist mountains in China. Traditionally it is considered to be the *bodhimaṇḍa* of Mañjuśrī Bodhisattva.

# *Hung-chou Shui-lao*

(For the story of the Shui-lao's awakening, see the *Record of Ma-tsu,* dialogue 16.)

Once a monk drew a circle and placed it on the Master's body with his hands. The Master shook it off thrice; then he also drew a circle and pointed to the monk. The monk bowed; the Master hit him, saying, "You liar!"

*

Someone asked the Master, "What is the practice of a *śramaṇa?"*

The Master said, "When there is a movement, a shadow appears; with awareness, ice forms."

*

Someone asked, "What is the great meaning of Buddhadharma?" The Master clapped his hands and laughed heartily. Whenever students came to him, he responded in a similar way.

# *Layman P'ang-yün*

Layman P'ang-yün (d. 808) was a native of Heng-yang in Heng- chou.[1] Raised in a Confucian environment, when he came of age, he got married and had a son and a daughter. Sometime during the middle of his life he threw all of his wealth into a river and decided to dedicate himself to religious life. His whole family shared his enthusiasm about Buddhism, and his daughter Ling-chao gained deep understanding of Ch'an. He first studied with Shih-t'ou; later he went to stay with Ma-tsu, under whom he had his main awakening. During the later part of his life he made a number of pilgrimages on which he visited many of the famous Ch'an masters of the time. He left a number of poems which reflect his deep insight into Buddhism.

*

One day Shih-t'ou asked the layman, "Since you saw me last time, how has your daily activity been?"

The layman replied, "If you ask me about my daily activity, I have nothing really to say."

Then he presented a verse, which says:

My daily activity is not different,
It is only that I am spontaneously in harmony with it;
Not grasping or rejecting anything,
Everywhere there is nothing to assert or oppose.
Whose are the titles of vermillion and purple?[2]
The mountain is without a speck of dust.
Supernatural powers and wonderful activity:
Fetching water and carrying firewood.

Shih-t'ou approved of it.

*

The layman had two verses, which say:

When the mind is thus, objects are also thus:
Not real and not unreal.
Not concerning oneself with existence,
And not dwelling in nothingness;
Not a saint,
Just an ordinary man who has done his job.

and,

Easy, really easy!
These five *skandhas* have true wisdom.
In the whole universe there is the same One Vehicle;[3]
How can in the formless *dharmakāya* there be two?
If you try to reject passions in order to enter *bodhi,*
I don't know where will the Buddha stage be.

**NOTES:**

1. Heng-yang is in present-day Hunan province. Another record says that he was born in Hsian-yang, in present-day Hupeh province, and that his family moved to Heng-yang during his early childhood. See R. F. Sasaki et al., *The Recorded Sayings of Layman P'ang* (Weatherhill: New York, 1971), p. 39.

2. Vermilion and purple were the colors of the dress worn by high officials during the T'ang Dynasty.

3. The phrase "One Vehicle" refers to the ultimate teaching of Buddhism, or rather the universal reality of it, as opposed to the provisional teachings of the three vehicles. The most popular scriptural assertion of the One Vehicle in East Asia is presented in the *Lotus Sūtra*.

# *Kuei-tsung Chih-ch'ang*

The Master said, "From the past the ancient worthies were not without knowledge and understanding. Those men of exalted characters were not the same as the common lot. Nowadays, because people lack attainment of their own and are not independent, they spend their time in vain. All of you—do not use your minds wrongly! There is no one who can do it for you, nor is there any place for you to use your minds. Don't seek from others—it is because you have always been relying on other people's understanding that whatever is said, it becomes a hindrance and the light can not penetrate. It is like having something in front of your eyes [so that you cannot see other objects]."

*

A monk asked, "What is the profound purport?"

The Master said, "There is no one who can understand that."

The monk asked, "How should one approach it?"

The Master said, "If one tries to approach it, one goes away from it."

The monk asked, "And what if one does not approach it?"

The Master said, "Then who is seeking the profound purport?" Then he added, "Go away! This is not something you should think about."

The monk said, "How could it be that you have no expedient teaching to lead me to enter [into it]?"

The Master said, "The power of Kuan-yin's subtle wisdom can save the world from suffering."[1]

The monk asked, "What is the power of the Kuan-yin's subtle wisdom?"

The Master hit the lid of the tripod three times, and asked "Do you hear?"

The monk said, "I hear."

The Master asked, "How is it that I don't hear?" The monk could not answer. The Master chased him away with his stick.

*

The Master and Nan-ch'üan used to practice together, until one day they suddenly separated. Once, while they were making tea, Nan- ch'üan asked, "I already understand a number of things we have discussed in the past. Later on, if someone asks you about the ultimate matter, what are you going to say?"

The Master said, "This piece of land is excellent for a hut."

Nan-ch'üan said, "Let's leave that hut aside; what are you going to say about the ultimate matter?"

The Master broke the teapot and got up. Nan-ch'üan said, "My elder Dharma-brother finished his tea; I still haven't had mine."

The Master said, "With that kind of talk, you will not be able to digest even a drop of water."

*

Once the Master went into the garden while [the monks] were picking vegetables. He drew a circle around one of the plants and told the monks, "Don't move this." None of the monks dared to touch it.

After a while, the Master came back, and when he

saw that the vegetables were still there, he chased the monks with his stick, saying, "What a bunch; none of you has any wisdom!"

*

Once, as a monk was taking leave of the Master, the Master called him, "Come closer; I am going to teach you the Buddhadharma." The monk drew closer; the Master told him, "All of you are bound by things. Come back some other time; then no one will know you. The weather is cold; have a nice trip. Now go!"

*

Once, on the occasion of giving a formal talk, the Master said, "Now I am going to speak about Ch'an; all of you come closer." The monks mover forward. The Master said, "Have you heard about Kuan-yin's activity which appropriately responds [to the needs of beings] at all places?"

The monks asked, "What is Kuan-yin's activity?"

The Master snapped his fingers, and said, "Do you all hear?"

The monks said, "Yes, we hear."

The Master said, "This useless bunch! What are you looking for here?" He then chased them with his stick, and returned to his quarters laughing loudly.

*

A monk asked, "How should a beginner[2] obtain an entry [into the Path]?"

The Master hit the lid of the tripod three times, and asked, "Do you hear?"

The monk said, "Yes, I do."

The Master asked, "How is it that I cannot hear?"

The Master then hit [the lid] three times, and asked, "Do you hear?"

The monk said, "I don't."

The Master asked, "How is it that I can hear?" The monk had no reply. The Master said, "The power of Kuan-yin's wisdom can save the world from suffering."

*

When a certain monk was taking leave of the Master, the Master asked him, "Where are you going?"

The monk replied, "I am going to study the five flavors of Ch'an."[3]

The Master said, "Everywhere there is five-flavored Ch'an; here I have only one-flavored Ch'an."

The monk asked, "What is the one-flavored Ch'an like?" The Master hit the monk, who then exclaimed, "I understand! I understand!"

The Master demanded, "Speak! Speak!" As the monk was about to open his mouth [to say something], the Master hit him again.

Later on the same monk went to Huang-po and related to him the previous exchange. Huang-po then summoned the assembly, and after he brought this matter to the monks, he said, "Among the eighty-four teachers that came from among Ma-tsu's disciples, all of them are fumblers; it is only Kuei-tsung that goes beyond the rest."[4]

**NOTES:**

1. Kuan-yin is the Chinese rendering of the name of Avalokiteśvara, the Bodhisattva of compassion. He, or she, according to the needs of the situation appears in numerous forms through the world in order to alleviate the suffering of beings, and lead them towards the Buddha's Path of wisdom and compassion.

2. One who has just set his mind to seek unsurpassed enlightenment, and has not yet undergone all the stages of the Path.

3. The five flavors of Ch'an, or the five kinds of Ch'an (meditation) practice are: Ch'an of the non-Buddhist, of ordinary people, Hīnayāna practitioners, Mahāyāna practitioners, and the supreme Ch'an.

4. On another occasion Huang-po said: "Among the eighty-four disciples of Great Master Ma who sat at the site of enlightenment, the number of those who obtained Master Ma's proper eye does not go beyond two or three. Venerable Lu-shan was one of them." (CTL ***chüan*** 9, Huang-po's entry). Venerable Lu-shan is the name by which Kuei- tsung was known; it comes from the name of the mountain where he resided.

# *Appendix*

## Sources for the Translations

The *Record of Ma-tsu* presented in this volume is a translation of *Chiang-hsi ma-tsu tao-i ch'an-shih yü-lu (Record of the Sayings of Ch'an master Ma-tsu Tao-i of Kiangsi).* This work forms part of *Ssu-chia yü-lu (Records of Four Masters,* HTC vol. 119, p. 405c-409a). Parts of the same text can also be found in the *Transmission of the Lamp* (T vol. 51, p. 245c-246c) and *Ku tsun-su yü-lu* (HTC vol. 118, p. 159b-161b). I have used the last two texts only when the primary text was obviously in error, of which there are only a few instances. Other early works which include materials about Ma-tsu are *Tsu-tang chi,* p. 260-265, and *Sung kao-seng chuan* (T vol. 50, p. 766a-c). These two works have not been extensively utilized for the present volume and have only occasionally been alluded to in the notes.

Most of the translations from the records of Ma-tsu's disciples that appear in part three of this volume have been translated from the *Transmission of the Lamp,* with the exceptions of Pai-chang and Nan-ch'üan. Pai-chang's dialogues with Ma-tsu can be found in *Ku tsun-su yü-lu,* and his sermons in *Ssu-chia yü-lu.* Nan-ch'üan's sermon is translated from his entry in *Ku tsun-su yü-lu.* The biographical information that precede the teachings of some of Ma-tsu's disciples have been drawn primarily from the *Transmission of the Lamp* and *Sung kao-seng chuan.* Absence of biographical information implies that no such information is available.

Various English translations of parts of this volume's translations have previously appeared in different publications. Those works which I have consulted when doing the present translations are: John Blofeld, *The Zen Teaching of Instantaneous Awakening*, for the chapter on Ta-chu; Chang Chung-yuan, *Original Teachings of Ch'an Buddhism*, for some of the chapters on Ma-tsu's disciples and parts of the *Record*; Thomas Cleary, *Sayings and Doings of Pai-chang*, for the material dealing with Pai-chang; Peigwang Li, "The Recorded Sayings of Ma-tzu Tao-i," for the *Record*; Charles Luk, *The Transmission of the Mind Outside of the Teaching*, for the chapter on Pai-chang and parts of the *Record*; Sohaku Ogata, *The Transmission of the Lamp: Early Masters*, for some of the material from the *Transmission of the Lamp*; and R. F. Sasaki, et al., *The Recorded Sayings of Layman P'ang*, for the material dealing with P'ang-yün.

# *Glossary*

*aggregates:* see *five skandhas.*

*Bhagavat:* "the Holy One," "the World-honored One," one of the epithets of a Buddha.

*bhikṣu:* fully ordained Buddhist monk.

*bodhi:* enlightenment, awakening; the realization of reality.

*bodhimaṇḍa:* "place of enlightenment," a place or sphere in which the enlightened mind manifests itself.

*Bodhisattva:* a being who is fully dedicated to the goal of complete enlightenment and universal liberation.

*Buddha:* someone who has achieved perfect enlightenment; the Reality itself.

*Buddhadharma:* see *Dharma.*

*Buddha-nature:* the pure, unalloyed, luminous essence of the mind of all sentient beings.

*chüan:* a division of a book; used in classical Chinese works.

*dhāraṇī:* mystical invocation, spell, mantra.

*Dharma:* ultimate truth, reality as perceived by a Buddha; the teachings that lead to personal realization of that reality; (when lowercased) elemental entities that make phenomena; any phenomena—thing, event, concept, idea, etc..

*dharmadhātu:* the "Dharma-element," or the "realm of reality"; according to different contexts it can mean both the essential nature from which arise both the absolute and the realm of phenomenal appearances, and the universe as it is perceived by the Buddha.

*Dharma-eye:* the eye of truth that perceives reality.

*dharmakāya:* dharma-body, the absolute aspect of reality, the essence of Buddhahood which is identical in all Buddhas; one of the three bodies of a Buddha.

*Dharma-nature:* *dharmatā*, the absolute nature underlying all phenomena; the Reality. Often used as a synonym for Nirvāṇa, Buddha-nature, suchness, etc..

*five skandhas*: sometimes referred to as the "five aggregates," are *rūpa,* or physical form; *vedanā,* sensation, feeling; *sañjñā,* conception; *saṃskāra,* volition, impulses of like and dislike; *vijñāna,* consciousness. These are the physical and mental constituents, the combination of which creates the phenomenal.

*Hīnayāna:* the "small vehicle" of those who pursue the path of individual salvation and consider the ending of defiling mental tendencies to be complete liberation.

*kalpa:* eon, age, immensely long period of time.

*karma:* any physical, verbal, or mental activity that produces a result; the universal law that every action brings consequences that are largely determined by the nature of that action.

*Mahāyāna:* the "Great Vehicle" that reveals the complete liberation of all sentient beings; Bodhisattva's Path of universal salvation.

*Māra:* demon; personification of forces, both internal and external, that obscure the true nature and lead one away from the Buddha's Path.

*Middle Way*: the way between the two extremes of existence and nothingness which reveals the Reality of all things.

*mind-ground:* the pivotal basis of the mind, from which all things spring.

*mind-seal:* synonym for the Buddha-mind present in all beings.

*Nirvāṇa:* complete liberation characterized by absence of delusion and permanent bliss; perfect quiescence.

*One Vehicle:* see *vehicle.*

*Parinirvāṇa:* the state of perfect quiescence entered by a Buddha upon the dissolution of his physical body.

*prajñā:* transcendent wisdom, non-discursive immediate perception of the way things truly are.

*samādhi:* state of mental imperturbability and clarity, meditative absorption.

*saṃsāra:* the cycle of birth and death.

*saṅgha:* the community of Buddhist monks (*bhikṣu*) and nuns (*bhikṣuṇī*); the idealized community of Buddhist saints.

*śarīra:* relic, especially of a Buddhist saint.

*śāstra:* commentary on a sūtra; treatise on Buddhist philosophy.

*śīla:* precepts, moral observances, virtuous behavior.

*śramaṇa:* Buddhist monk or nun, a recluse.

*Śrāvaka:* "hearer," a disciple of the Buddha who understands the basic teachings and follows the path of individual liberation.

*śūnyatā:* lack of permanent self-existing nature in all things. All things are relative and depend on sets of external causes and conditions for their existence. Often translated as "voidness," or "emptiness."

*sūtra:* Buddhist scripture, text which is considered to contain the actual teachings of the Buddha.

*Tathāgata:* "one who has come from suchness," one of the epithets of a Buddha.

*tathāgatagarbha:* "embryo of the Tathāgata," or "womb of the Tathāgata"; mind's inherent enlightenment which represents the potential of every living being to become a Buddha.

*ten stages:* the stages of the Bodhisattva Path, which according to the *Avataṃsaka Sūtra* are: joy, freedom from defilement, effulgence, blazing wisdom, hard to conquer, appearance, proceeding far, unmovable, virtuous wisdom, cloud of Dharma.

*three realms:* the realm of desire, the realm of form, and the formless realm. Also known as the "three worlds."

*tripiṭaka:* the Buddhist canon in which all scriptures are arranged into three divisions: sūtras, Vinaya, and *śāstras*.

*vehicle:* simile for the Buddha's teaching which carries over all living beings to enlightenment and liberation. The two vehicles are the vehicles of the *śrāvakas* and *Pratyekabuddhas* (self-enlightened ones). The three vehicles are these two plus the vehicle of the Bodhisattvas. These three are said to be expedient soteriological contrivances; it is only the One (Buddha) Vehicle that completely discloses the ultimate reality.

*Vinaya:* monastic discipline, rules that regulate the monastic life.

# *Bibliography*

**Classical Works:**


*Ch'an-men kuei-shih.* In CTL *chüan* 6.
*Ch'an-yüan chu-ch'üan-chi tu-hsü.* T 2015. vol. 48.
*Chao lun.* T 1858. vol. 45.
*Cheng fa-yen tsang.* HTC vol. 118.
*Cheng-tao ko.* In CTL *chüan* 30.
*Ching-te ch'uan-teng lu.* T 2076. vol. 51; also Taipei: Hsin wen-feng ch'u-pan kung-ssu, 1988.
*Ch'uan hsin fa-yao.* Taipei: Fo-chiao ch'u-pan she, 1984.
*Chung-hua ch'üan hsin-ti ch'an-men shih-tzu ch'eng-hsi t'u.* HTC vol. 110.
*Fa-chu ching.* T 2901. vol. 85.
*Hsü kao-seng chuan.* T 2060. vol. 50.
*Hsin-hsin ming.* In CTL *chüan* 30; also T 2010. vol. 48.
*Hsiu hua-yen ching ao-chih wang-chin huan yüan kuan.* T 1876. vol. 45.
*Li-tai fa-pao chi.* T 2075. vol.51.
*Kao-seng chuan.* T 2059. vol. 50.
*Kuei-shan ching-ts'e.* HTC vol. 111.
*Ku tsun-su yü-lu.* HTC vol. 118.
*Pi-yen lu.* T 2003. vol. 48.
*Ssu-chia yü-lu.* HTC vol. 119.
*Sung kao-seng chuan.* T 2061. vol. 50.
*Ta-fang-kuang fo hua-yen ching.* T 278. vol. 9, and T 279. vol. 10.
*Ta-sheng ch'i-hsin lun.* T 1666. vol. 32.
*Tsu-tang chi.* Taipei: Kuang-wen shu-chu, 1972.
*Tsung-ching lu.* T 2016. vol. 48.
*Tsung-men shih-kuei lun.* HTC vol. 110.
*Yüan-chueh ching ta-shu ch'ao.* HTC vol. 14, and vol. 15.

**Modern Works:**

Blofeld, John, trans. *The Zen Teaching of Huang-po on the Transmission of Mind.* New York: Grove Press, 1958.

———, trans. *The Zen Teaching of Instantaneous Awakening.* Leicester: Buddhist Publishing Group, 1987. (Originally published as *The Zen Teaching of Hui Hai on Sudden Illumination.* London: Rider & Company, 1962.)

Broughton, Jeffrey. "K'uei-feng Tsung-mi: Convergence of Ch'an and the Teaching." Ph.D. diss., Columbia University, 1975.

Buswell, Robert E., trans. *The Korean Approach to Zen: The Collected Works of Chinul.* Honolulu: University of Hawaii Press, 1983.

———. *The Formation of Ch'an Ideology in China and Korea:* The Vajra Samadhi Sutra, *A Buddhist Apocriphon.* Princeton: Princeton University Press, 1989.

———, ed. *Chinese Buddhist Apocrypha.* Honolulu: University of Hawaii Press, 1990.

Chang Chung-yuan, trans. *Original Teachings of Ch'an Buddhism.* New York: Vintage Books, 1971.

Chappel, David W., ed. *T'ien-t'ai Buddhism: An Outline of the Fourfold Teachings.* Tokyo: Daiichi Shobo, 1983.

———. "The Teachings of the Fourth Patriarch Tao-hsin (580-658)," in Whalen Lai and Lewis R. Lancaster, eds. *Early Ch'an in China and Tibet.* Berkeley Buddhist Studies Series, no. 5, Berkeley: Asian Humanities Press, 1983.

———, ed. *Buddhist and Taoist Practice in Medieval Chinese Society.* Asian Studies at Hawaii, No. 34. Honolulu: University of Hawaii Press, 1987.

Ch'en, Kenneth. *Buddhism in China: A Historical Survey.* Princeton: Princeton University Press, 1964.

———. *The Chinese Transformation of Buddhism.* Princeton: Princeton University Press, 1973.

Cleary, J.C., trans. *Zen Dawn: Early Zen Texts from Tung Huang*. Boston & London: Shambhala Publications, 1986.

———, trans. *Zibo: The Last Great Zen Master of China*. Berkeley: Asian Humanities Press, 1989.

———, trans. *Swampland Flowers: Letters and Lectures of Zen Master Ta Hui*. New York: Grove Press, 1977.

Cleary, Thomas, trans. *Sayings and Doings of Pai-chang*. Los Angeles: Center Publications, 1978.

———, trans. *The Flower Ornament Scripture*. 3 vols. Boston & London: Shambhala Publications, 1984-1987.

———. *Entry Into the Inconceivable: An Introduction to Hua-yen Buddhism*. Honolulu: University of Hawaii Press, 1983.

Cleary, Thomas, and J.C. Cleary, trans. *The Blue Cliff Record*. 3 vols. Boulder: Shambhala Publications, 1977.

Collcutt, Martin. "The early Ch'an Monastic Rule: *Ch'ing kuei* and the shaping of Ch'an Community Life," in Whalen Lai and Lewis Lancaster, eds. *Early Ch'an in China and Tibet*. Berkeley Buddhist Series, no. 5. Berkeley: Asian Humanities Press, 1983.

———. *Five Mountains: The Rinzai Zen Monastic Institution in Medieval Japan*. Cambridge: Harvard University Press, 1981.

Dumoulin, Henrich. *Zen Buddhism: A History*. 2 vols. New York: Macmillan Publishing Company, 1988.

Foulk, Theodore Griffit. "The Ch'an School and its Place in the Buddhist Monastic Tradition." Ph.D. diss., University of Michigan, Ann Arbor, 1987.

Gimello, Robert M. "Chih-yen (602-668) and the Foundation of Hua-yen Buddhism." Ph.D. diss., Columbia University, 1976.

Gimello, Robert M., and Peter Gregory, eds. *Studies in Ch'an and Hua Yen*. Studies in East Asian Buddhism, no. 1. Honolulu: University of Hawaii Press, 1983.

Gregory, Peter N., ed. *Sudden and Gradual: Approaches to*

*Enlightenment in Chinese Thought.* Studies in East Asian Buddhism, no. 5. Honolulu: University of Hawaii Press, 1987.

Hakeda, Yoshito S., trans. *The Awakening of Faith.* New York: Columbia University Press, 1967.

Hu Shih. "Hsin chiao-ting-te tung-huang hsieh-pen shen-hsiu ho-shang i-chu liang chung," in *Ch'an-tsung tien-chi yen-chiu.* Hsien-tai fo-chiao hsüeh-shu ts'ung-k'an, no. 12, Taipei: Ta-sheng wen-hua ch'u-pan she, 1977.

Hurvitz, Leon. "Chih-i (538-597): An Introduction to the Life and Ideas of a Chinese Buddhist Monk." *Melanges Chinois et Bouddhiques* 12 (1962) p. 1-372.

Jan Yun-hua. *Tsung-mi.* Taipei: Tung ta t'u-shu kung-ssu yin-hsing, 1988.

———. "Tsung-mi: His Analysis of Ch'an Buddhism." *T'oung Pao* 58 (Leiden, 1972) p. 1-54.

———. "Conflict and Harmony in Ch'an Buddhism." *Journal of Chinese Philosophy* 4 (1977) p. 287-302.

Lai, Whalen, and Lewis Lancaster, eds. *Early Ch'an in China and Tibet.* Berkeley Buddhist Series, no. 5. Berkeley: Asian Humanities Press, 1983.

Luk, Charles, trans. *The Vimalakirti Nirdesa Sutra.* Boston & Shaftesbury: Shambhala, 1990.

———, trans. *The Transmission of the Mind Outside of the Teaching.* New York: Grove Press, 1975.

Keel Hee-sung. *Chinul: The Founder of the Korean Son Tradition.* Berkeley Buddhist Studies Series, no. 6. Seoul: Po Chin Chai, 1984.

McRae, John R. *The Northern School and the Formation of Early Ch'an Buddhism.* Studies in East Asian Buddhism, no. 3. Honolulu: University of Hawaii Press, 1986.

———. "The Ox-head School of Chinese Ch'an Buddhism: From early Ch'an to the Golden Age," in Robert M.

Gimello and Peter Gregory, eds. *Studies in Ch'an and Hua Yen*, Studies in East Asian Buddhism, no. 1. Honolulu: University of Hawaii Press, 1983.

Powell, William, trans. *The Record of Tung-shan* . Honolulu: University of Hawaii Press, 1986.

Red Pine, trans. *The Zen Teaching of Bodhidharma.* San Francisco: North Point Press, 1989.

Reischauer, Edwin O. *Ennin's Travels In T'ang China.* New York: Ronald Press, 1955.

———, trans. *Ennin's Diary: The Record of a Pilgrimage to China in Search of the Law.* New York: Ronald Press, 1955.

Schloegl, Irmgard, trans. *The Zen Teaching of Rinzai.* Berkeley: Shambhala Publications, 1976.

Sohaku Ogata, trans. *The Transmission of the Lamp: Early Masters.* Wolfeboro: Longwood Academic, 1990.

Song-chol, Ven. *Echoes from Mt. Kaya.* Seoul: Lotus Lantern International Buddhist Center, 1988.

Suzuki, Daisetz Teitaro, trans. *The Laṅkāvatāra Sūtra.* Boulder: Prajna Press, 1978 (Originaly published in 1932 by Routledge & Kegan Paul Ltd).

Swanson, Paul. *Foundation of T'ien-t'ai Philosophy.* Berkeley: Asian Humanities Press, 1989.

Takemoto, Melvin M. "The Kuei-shan ching-ts'e: Morality in the Hung-chou School of Ch'an." M.A. thesis, University of Hawaii, 1983.

Weinstein, Stanley. *Buddhism under the T'ang.* Cambridge: Cambridge University Press, 1987.

Welch, Holmes. *The Practice of Chinese Buddhism: 1900-1950.* Cambridge: Harvard University Press, 1975.

Yampolsky, Philip B., trans. *The Platform Sutra of the Sixth Patriarch.* New York: Columbia University Press, 1967.

Yanagida, Seizan. "The *Li-tai fa-pao chi* and the Ch'an Doctrine of Sudden Awakening," translated by Carl W.

Bielefeldt, in Whalen Lai and Lewis Lancaster, eds. *Early Ch'an in China and Tibet*, Berkeley Buddhist Series, no. 5. Berkeley: Asian Humanities Press, 1983.

Yang Hsüan Chih. *A Record of Buddhist Monasteries in Lo-yang*. trans. by Wang Yi-t'ung. Princeton: Princeton University Press, 1984.

Yin Shun. *Chung-kuo ch'an-tsung shih*. Taipei: Cheng-wen ch'u-pan she, 1983.

Zurcher, E. *The Buddhist Conquest of China*. 2 vols. Leiden: E.J. Brill, 1959.